DATE DUE

Demco, Inc. 38-293

WEST'S LAW SCHOOL
ADVISORY BOARD

ADOPTION LAWS
IN A NUTSHELL

By

SANFORD N. KATZ
Darald and Juliet Libby Professor of Law
Boston College Law School

DANIEL R. KATZ, Esq.
Member, Bars of Massachusetts, New York,
California and the District of Columbia

WEST®
A Thomson Reuters business

Nutshell Series, In a Nutshell and the Nutshell Logo are trademarks registered in the U.S. Patent and Trademark Office.

© 2012 Thomson Reuters

    610 Opperman Drive
    St. Paul, MN 55123
    1–800–313–9378

Printed in the United States of America

ISBN: 978–0–314–19030–7

For
Joan

PREFACE AND
ACKNOWLEDGMENTS

The laws regulating the formation of family relationships like marriage, civil unions, domestic partnerships and adoption are found in state statutes and may differ considerably from jurisdiction to jurisdiction. There may be a variety of reasons for this phenomenon including the religious, political and ethnic make-up of the citizens of the jurisdiction. History plays an important role as well. American adoption laws, for example, do not trace their origins back to the English common law, like so many of American laws, but have a distinct American foundation. Because of the lack of homogeneity in the population of the United States, and because adoption is so reflective of a jurisdiction's social policy, the laws of adoption in the United States lack uniformity, and attempts to establish a uniform law of adoption have been unsuccessful. It is for that reason that one cannot accurately speak of American adoption law. Rather, one must refer to the American laws of adoption. This is why the title of this book is *Adoption Laws in a Nutshell*. This is also why we have included charts that present the law of each jurisdiction on the subject of the chart.

We caution the reader to check the current state of the law since the charts were developed from 2009 to 2012 and some changes may have occurred since then. We also alert the reader to the fact that the laws regarding intercountry adoption may also change.

A number of Boston College Law School students assisted in the development of the charts and also did research on specific topics. We acknowledge with appreciation the work of Stephanie Giuliano Abhar, Tarek Audi, Michael Avery, Andrew Bender, Mark DeVincentis, Kevin Gallagher, Andrew Jones, Sam Lawrence, Julie Meeks, Michael Mohr, Feyisara Olotu, Ryan M. Rourke–Reed, Victoria Santoro, Peter Tipps, Paul Wagoner, Christine Weaver, Barrett Wilson–Murphy and Ben Winterhalter. Special thanks are due Meg Parsont for her excellent editing and Curtis Beyer for his valuable technical assistance in preparing the manuscript for publication.

The Bibliography consists of sources for the information in this book and suggestions for further reading in specific areas.

OUTLINE

OUTLINE

TABLE OF CASES

References are to Pages

TABLE OF CASES

Estate of (see name of party)

TABLE OF CASES

ADOPTION LAWS

IN A NUTSHELL

INTRODUCTION

State statutory laws regulating the adoption of children under the age of eighteen have as their origin the Massachusetts Act to Provide for the Adoption of Children, (MASS. REV. STAT. ch. 324 (Supp. 1851)) which was enacted in 1851. The Act differed from the model of adoption law in the past by its providing for a judicial proceeding to adopt a child rather than a private informal agreement, deed, or a legislative act to formally change the name of a child and secure the child's right to inheritance. In addition, the adoption process, rather than a transaction or a legislative act, took into account the welfare of the child to be adopted and the qualifications and fitness of the adults who were to become the adoptive parents. From 1851 until 1873, the legislatures of Pennsylvania, Indiana, Georgia, Wisconsin, Ohio, Michigan, New Hampshire, Oregon, Connecticut, Kansas, California, Maine, Rhode Island, North Carolina and New York enacted adoption statutes. They followed the lead of Massachusetts in providing judicial regulation of a process that sought to advance a child's welfare.

The Massachusetts Act predated the English law of adoption enacted by Parliament in 1926 by slightly over seventy-five years. The reasons ordinarily given for the timing of the English adoption

1

law have centered on the low birth rate at that time, deaths of men in World War I and the war's devastating impact on families, adult deaths caused by the influenza epidemic, and the resulting orphaned and abandoned child population. In a way, the English adoption law was designed to protect those children and legalize the informal practice of parenting them.

Throughout the history of American adoption laws there has been a tension between focusing on the adoptive parents' motivation, for example creating a family for childless couples and providing them with heirs, and the interests and needs of the child, namely, providing the child with a family. In addition, there has also been conflict between giving rights to adopted children identical to those who were not adopted on the one hand, and limiting those rights, especially in regard to inheritance, on the other.

Adoption both in law and in practice in the nineteenth and twentieth centuries was different from what it is in the twenty-first century. It can no longer be divided into two processes: the formal and voluntary relinquishment of a child to a prospective adoptive couple or to a licensed adoption agency for placement or the involuntary termination of parental rights to a child and the subsequent adoption of that child by the child's foster parents or others. While both those processes exist, new artificial reproductive techniques with all their possibilities have provided another source for adoption. This method of reproduction has become particularly attractive to individuals and couples seeking adoption in the twenty-first century as domestic and international sources for adoptable children decrease. That decrease has been caused by the decline in the domestic birth rate, the change in attitudes toward the pregnancy of single women who may raise their children themselves or have them raised by relatives and the restrictions by foreign countries in exporting children for adoption.

In addition, while in the past it could have been said that the adoption decree terminates all legal and custodial rights of the birth parents to their children, and seals the adoption records from individual and public view, such statements can no longer be asserted absolutely. For example, as we shall see later, adoption may not sever all inheritance rights either of the adopted child from his birth parents or the birth parents from the adopted child. Individual state statutes must be consulted. In addition, a birth parent's custodial rights under certain circumstances may survive the adoption in a limited way. Perhaps the most remarkable change in both adoption law and practice over the past fifty to one hundred years has been the removal of the shield of secrecy that covered adoption and the social taboo that restricted its open discussion.

Children available for adoption may come from local communities, other American jurisdictions or foreign countries. If a child is brought into a state from another state for purposes of adoption, the

Interstate Compact on the Placement of Children, enacted in all American jurisdictions, must be complied with. Lawyers who are counseling prospective adoptive parents are advised to consult the Guide to the Interstate Compact on Placement of Children. If the ICPC is violated, the violator (the adoptive parents, their lawyer or the sending agency that was involved in the placement) may be subject to civil or criminal sanctions. A severe result of noncompliance could result in the adoption petition being dismissed.

State adoption statutes vary as to the substantive law as well as the proper court to handle adoptions, those being either courts of general jurisdiction or specialized courts such as a probate court or a family court. In addition, like other areas of family law, there may be a specific residency requirement for persons seeking adoption. That requirement may vary from sixty days to one year, depending on the jurisdiction. In addition, actual or constructive notice of the adoption hearing must be given to all interested parties.

The reason for the lack of uniformity in state laws regulating adoption may lie with the desire of individual state officials to have its law reflect its state's own social policies regarding children. There was a reluctance on the part of state legislatures to enact the Uniform Adoption Act, originally proposed in 1951, later to be withdrawn and a 1994 Act replacing it. Only Alaska, Arkansas, Montana,

North Dakota, Ohio and Oklahoma enacted some version of the 1951 Act.

This book is divided into four parts: Part One: Establishing the Adoptive Relationship; Part Two: Maintaining the Adoptive Relationship; and Part Three: Special Federal Legislation; and Part Four: Intercountry Adoption.

PART ONE

ESTABLISHING THE ADOPTIVE RELATIONSHIP

I. Voluntary System

A. Independent or Private Placements

The conventional approach to adoption, which had as its goal the provision of a childless couple with a child, was the birth mother's relinquishment of her child to that couple either directly or through a third party like a lawyer, physician or clergyman. That approach, which empowered the birth mother to make her own decision as to who would raise her child, is called independent or private adoption. Even with private placement, the prospective adoptive parents must secure judicial approval. Usually that approval follows an informal judicial hearing which includes a court-ordered assessment or home study of the adoptive parent if one has not been conducted by a licensed adoption agency. An assessment or home study typically involves an examination of the prospective adoptive parents including the circumstances surrounding the couple's meeting, their marriage and how the couple relates to each other, their family background, their relations with family members, their physical and emotional health, work history, financial situation and their reputation and participation in their community. The study may also include an examination of the living arrangement to determine whether plans for the adopted child are appropriate in terms of living space. A home study may take weeks to complete to allow for documentation of certain facts and communication with references. Ordinarily a home study will include a recommendation by the person who has conducted the study as to the appropriateness of the adoption for the particular applicant.

If the judge finds that the court papers are properly completed with no objectionable information—such as an exchange of money that would in any way suggest that the child has been sold and the home study reveals that the prospective adoptive couple would be suitable parents, the judge issues an adoption decree. A home study may be waived in the case of a step-parent adoption or a kinship adoption. Kinship adoption describes the adoption by the adopted child's relatives like her birth grandparents, her aunts or uncles. Ordinarily, for the home study waiver to be effective the child must have lived with his/her step-parent or relative for a certain length of time. In addition, in Florida, for example, grandparents are given priority in the adoption of their grandchild if the grandchild has lived with them for six months. (FLA. STAT. § 63.0425 (1)) Unlike other judicial decrees, adoption decrees are ordinarily not open for public inspection.

It should be noted that as a decree, the adoption decree should be recognized in a sister jurisdiction under the Full Faith and Credit Clause of the U. S. Constitution. This is particularly important with regard to inheritance rights of the adopted child. There is no uniformity among the jurisdictions on how foreign adoption decrees are treated in the United States. For the most part, a foreign country adoption is recognized in American courts so long as it has been verified and approved by the Immigration and Naturalization Services. Some state laws require that the foreign adoption not offend the state's public policies. The state in which the adoptive couple resides determines whether the foreign adoption decree is satisfactory and whether a local proceeding, like re-adoption, is necessary. Intercountry adoptions are discussed later in this book.

Those who promote private adoptions often base their position on the ground that such adoptions support a birth mother's right to place her child with whomever she wishes. To the argument that such a right might not be in the child's best interests, is the response that the court, in particular the judge's inquiry and the court-ordered home study of the prospective adoptive parent or parents, can provide the safety net. This may be true. However, unless a state statute provides that an adoption must occur within a certain time frame after placement, a child might reside with her prospective adoptive parents for months before the adoption petition is filed. For example, a petition for adoption in California must be filed within sixty days of the

adoptees' placement if the child is under the age of
one and within one hundred and twenty days if the
child is over the age of one. (CAL. FAM. CODE § 8911);
Vermont requires a petition to be filed no later than
forty-five days of placement. (VT. STAT. ANN. tit 15 A
§ 3–302). During that time the child might bond
with her adoptive parents and a judicial denial of
adoption, perhaps due to the fact that money did
change hands between the birth mother and the
prospective adoptive couple, could present a hard-
ship to the child. In addition, if a judge were to deny
the adoption, what would happen to the child if the
birth mother, relying on the belief that she has
placed her child with suitable parents, disappears?

A major problem with private adoptions is the
lack of backup that licensed adoption agencies provide. For example, in the case of a judge's denial of
an adoption as stated above, the placing agency
would be available to take the child back. But such
a situation would be rare because an agency placement process, if conducted properly and completely,
would reveal any deficiencies in the applicant's capacity to raise the adoptive child.

B. Agency Adoptions

The social work profession, especially its clinical
social workers, has a long and distinguished history
of treating children and adults as individuals or as a
group who may be having difficulties coping with
personal issues. Professional social workers (those
with graduate degrees in social work) are educated
in the psychodynamics of everyday life, especially

with regard to personality and behavior disorders. They are trained in interviewing and therapeutic techniques. It is therefore appropriate that the social work profession has been responsible for providing adoption services. Social workers provide the staffs for adoption agencies. They help in the recruitment of prospective adoptive parents for hard to place children. They conduct the necessary investigations of the adoptive applicants and provide counseling to birth mothers and fathers who contemplate relinquishing their child for adoption. They are in a position to discuss alternatives to adoption, such as a birth mother raising her child herself, and refer the birth mother to other social service agencies that can provide appropriate services. These services may include housing, day care and employment. In addition, social workers are available to discuss the meaning and legal implications of signing a consent to adoption document, assuring that the consent is obtained freely, with knowledge of the consequences of relinquishment and within the legal time frame set by state statute. Social workers are available to continue counseling post-adoption. They are also available to adoptive children who may seek their services years after the placement, especially if the adoptive child wishes to locate her birth parents. The placing agency is also available to receive a child back from a failed adoptive placement.

In mandating that all non-relative and non-step-parent adoption placements be made by licensed social service agencies, states that restrict other

adoption placements to those agencies like Connecticut, Delaware, Kentucky, Massachusetts, Minnesota and Wisconsin are attempting to prevent baby
selling and black market adoptions. They are also
trying to assure that birth parents, children and
prospective adoptive parents receive the appropriate
services from professional social workers whose aim
is to advance a child's welfare. Licensed social service agencies have the added feature of a built-in
system of accountability which involves, when appropriate, supervision of social workers within the
agency and if necessary, consultation with members
of other professions outside of the agency like pediatricians, teachers and psychiatrists,.

The history of child welfare agencies in the United States in promoting the best interests of children
is, for the most part, positive. However, in the
nineteenth and early twentieth centuries, certain
child welfare agencies in Boston, New York City
and Philadelphia were involved in the most deceptive practices imaginable by rounding up children
thought to be homeless and shipping them off to the
Midwest and West by train where they were actually sold to farmers (often from auction blocks) so
that they could perform menial tasks, although the
expressed reason was for the children to be free of
the foul city air and experience the cleanliness and
openness of the West. In addition, it was thought
that the children would be raised in an environment
that would enhance their Christian heritage. The
result was a form of de facto adoption. Many of
these children were not abandoned by their immi-

grant parents nor were their parents necessarily Christian. Basically the children were kidnapped for involuntary servitude. It took years for these children to recognize what had happened to them and attempt to locate their birth parents. This bleak period of child welfare history is documented in books about the "Orphan Trains."

1. Wrongful Adoption

Adoption agencies are not perfect and it is possible that they can make mistakes in the placement of children for adoption. Wrongful adoption is a term used to describe the cause of action available to an adoptive couple for the agency's failure, whether negligently or intentionally, to disclose important facts about the child and her birth parents, like the child's health, the birth parents' genetic background or the circumstances surrounding the birth of the child. Some states have specific statutes that require agencies to provide information about the child to the prospective adoptive parents. Failure to do so may give the adoptive parents a statutory cause of action called wrongful adoption. The tort of wrongful adoption is basically an extension of the common law doctrine of fraud and was recognized in Ohio in 1986 with the case of *Burr v. Board of County Comm'rs*, 491 N.E.2d 1101 (Ohio 1986). The issue in that case concerned intentional misrepresentation and left open the matter of simple nondisclosure. The latter issue was dealt with by the California Court of Appeals in *Michael J. v. County of Los Angeles Department* of *Adoptions*, 201 Cal. App.3d 859 (1988) where the Court of Appeal of

California (2nd Appellate Dist.) held that deliberate concealment of material facts could also trigger a wrongful adoption action. In that case, ten years after the adoption the adoptive parents brought an action for intentional misrepresentation and fraudulent concealment of the severity of the medical condition of their adopted child who suffered from Sturge–Weber Syndrome, a congenital degenerative nerve disorder resulting in the child's suffering an epileptic seizure. In *Meracle v. Children's Service Society of Wisconsin*, 437 N.W.2d 532 (Wis. 1989), the Wisconsin Supreme Court held that a wrongful adoption claim can be brought by an adoptive parent against an agency for negligently misrepresenting the child's health. In that case the agency affirmatively misrepresented the child's risk of developing Huntington's disease, a fatal illness that took the life of the child's paternal grandmother. In discussing the disease with the adoptive parents at the time of placement, the agency described the seriousness of it and the fact that it was genetically transmitted between generations. The agency said that since the adopted child's birth father tested negative for the disease, the child was not likely to develop it. At age five, the child was diagnosed with the disease. Illinois recognized the tort of adoption agency fraud and negligence in *Roe v. Catholic Charities of the Diocese of Springfield*, 588 N.E.2d 354 (Ill. App. Ct. 1992) where the private agency did not reveal information about the child's severe emotional problems and intellectual limitations. Since those cases were decided, many states have enacted statutes that codify the necessity of disclosure of important facts about the child such as medical and genetic history. It should be noted however, that a successful wrongful adoption action against an adoption agency provides the adoptive parents with compensation and in certain cases punitive damages if the adoptive parents can prove with clear and convincing evidence that the agency deliberately disregarded the rights or safety of others, a standard set out in *M.H. v. Caritas Family Serv.*, 488 N.W.2d 282, 284 (Minn. 1992). Whether the specific action can be brought against the birth parent depends on the jurisdiction. Certainly, the birth parent could be sued for fraud if there is clear and convincing evidence of intentional deception on the part of the adoptive parent, although the likelihood of recovery against her is probably remote considering her financial situation and the difficulty in locating her.

Another action that could be brought against an agency if there were sufficient evidence is the intentional infliction of emotional distress. In order to support such a claim a parent would have to show that the agency was willful, wanton and malicious in either its affirmative deceptive statements or in its failure to disclose important medical and genetic information about the adopted child or his birth parents.

2. Annulling or Abrogating the Adoption

If a state statute permits it, adoptive parents may also seek to annul the adoption. Three states have enacted statutes that allow adopting parents to abrogate adoptions. California allows adopted parents to set aside a decree of adoption if the child develops a serious mental or physical condition that was known to the agency at the time of adoption, but not revealed to them. CAL. FAM. CODE § 9100 (2012). Kentucky allows adopted parents to annul an adoption decree, if the child "reveals definite traits of ethnological ancestry different from those of the adoptive parents." KY. REV. STAT. ANN. § 199.540 (West 2011). New York's statute allows the court to "open, vacate or set aside such order of adoption for fraud, newly discovered evidence or other sufficient cause." N.Y. DOM. REL. LAW § 114(3) (McKinney 2012). The New York statute has no statute of limitations for such an action, unlike both the California and Kentucky statutes which subject adopting parents to a five year statute of limitations. Such abrogation statutes are uncommon, as most states have statutes making it impossible to challenge an adoption decree after a set period of time.

(*See e. g.*, ARK. CODE ANN. § 9–9–216 (West 2011) (adoption decree cannot be challenged after one year on any grounds); COLO. REV. STAT. ANN. § 19–5–214 (West 2012) (adoption decree cannot be challenged after ninety days for a procedural or jurisdiction defect, and after one year for fraud); HAW. REV. STAT. § 578–12 (2011) (adoption decree can be challenged up to one year for good cause); S.D. CODIFIED LAWS § 25–6–21 (2004), *amended by 2012 South Dakota Laws Ch. 143 (HB 1266),* (adoption decree cannot be challenged after two years, except in cases of fraud)). For the most part, however, the result of an adoption decree is to bind the adopted child to his adoptive parents. In the words of the Supreme Judicial Court of Massachusetts: "Adoption should create a for better, for worse situation." *In re Adoption of a Minor,* 214 N.E.2d 281, 282 (Mass. 1966).

a. Duty to Disclose Information

State	Statute	Case
Alabama	No	No
Alaska	No	No
Arizona	"[T]he division or the agency . . . shall compile and provide to the prospective adoptive parents detailed written nonidentifying information including a health and genetic history and all nonidentifying information about the birth parents or members of a birth parent's family." ARIZ. REV. STAT. ANN. § 8–129 (A) (2012).	*Taeger v. Catholic Family and Community Services,* 995 P.2d 721 (Ariz. Ct. App. 1999).
Arkansas	No	No
California	"[T]he department or licensed	*Richard P. v. Vista Del mar*

State	Statute	Case
	agency that made a medical report shall provide a copy of the medical report to ... the adoptive parent of a person under the age of 18 years who has been adopted pursuant to this part." Ca. Fam. Code § 9202 (2012).	*Child Care Service,* 106 Cal. App.3d 860 (1980).
Colorado	"The state registrar shall also prescribe an updated medical history statement, that a birth parent may submit, with the completed contact preference form, to the state registrar ... Such medical history statement shall indicate that the birth parent is waiving confidentiality of any medical information supplied." Colo. Rev. Stat. § 19–5–305(1.5)(b) (2012).	*Collier v. Krane,* 763 F. Supp. 473 (D. Colo. 1991) (Plaintiffs sued state under a federal claim, § 1983, that their wrongful adoption claim was a violation of their Constitutional rights. Claim was rejected).
Connecticut	"The report shall indicate ... the	No

State	Statute	Case
	physical, mental, and genetic history of the child . . . the child's health status . . . the child's birth, neonatal, and other medical, psychological, psychiatric, and dental history information . . . a record of immunizations for the child . . . and the available results of medical, psychological, psychiatric and dental examinations of the child." CONN. GEN. STAT. § 45A–727 (B)(2) (2012).	
Delaware	No	No
District of Columbia	No	*Ferenc v. World Child, Inc.,* 977 F.Supp. 56 (D.C. 1997) (Court accepted that D.C. law would recognize the tort of wrongful adoption, under either an intentional or negligent theory. However, because of an ex-

State	Statute	Case
		culpatory contract provision, defendants were able to win motions for summary judgment in this case).
Florida	"It is unlawful for: any person or adoption entity under this chapter to: (1) knowingly provide false information; or (2) knowingly withhold material information." FLA. STAT. §§ 63.212(2)(a)(1) & (2) (2012).	*Ambrose v. Catholic Social Services*, 736 So.2d 146 (Fla. Dist. App. 1999).
Georgia	No	*Moore v. Department of Human Res.*, 469 S.E.2d 511 (1996) (Court ruled that Department of Human Resources could not be sued on the theory of an implied contract to provide an adoption free of legal entanglements).
Hawaii	"The department of health shall prepare a standard form . . . for the purpose of	No

State	Statute	Case
	perpetuating medical information on the natural parents of the adopted minor child. This form shall include a request for any information relating to the adopted child's potential genetic or other inheritable diseases or afflictions, including but not limited to known genetic disorders, inheritable diseases, and similar medical histories, if known, of the parents of the natural parents." HAW. REV. STAT. § 578–14.5 (a) (2011).	
Idaho	No	No
Illinois	"The agency ... involved in the adoption proceedings shall give in writing the following non-identifying information, if known, to the adoptive parents not later than the date of placement with the petition-	*Roe v. Catholic Charities of the Diocese of Springfield*, 588 N.E.2d 354 (Ill. App. Ct. 1992).

State	Statute	Case
	ing adoptive parents:. . . (viii) detailed medical and mental health histories of the child, the biological parents, and their immediate relatives."	
	750 ILL COMP. STAT. 50/18.4(a) (2011).	
Indiana	"The state registrar: (1) shall release a copy of the medical history to any interested person; (2) may release a copy of the medical history to any person who satisfies the registrar that the person has a legitimate need; and (3) shall supplement the medical history with medical information received from any person."	No
	IND. CODE § 31–19–20–1(Sec. 1) (2011).	
Iowa	"[T]he department may allow access to adoption records . . . if . . . the person gain-	*Engstrom v. State*, 461 N.W.2d 309 (Iowa 1990).

State	Statute	Case
	ing access to the records uses them solely for the purposes of conducting a legitimate medical research project or of treating a patient in a medical facility.'' IOWA CODE § 600.24 (2012).	
Kansas	''The following information shall be filed with the petition in an independent or agency adoption: (1) A complete written genetic, medical and social history of the child and the parents . . . (3) any hospital records pertaining to the child or a properly executed authorization for release of those records.'' KAN. STAT. ANN. § 59–2130(a) (2012).	No
Kentucky	''[T]he health history and other nonidentifying background information of biological parents and blood relatives of	No

State	Statute	Case
	the adopted person . . . shall be given to the cabinet or child-placing agency which has the information to the adoptive parents . . . this information shall include the results of any tests for HIV or hepatitis A, B, and C." KY. REV. STAT. ANN. § 199.520 (4)(a) (2011).	
Louisiana	No	*April v. Associated Catholic Charities of New Orleans*, 629 So. 2d 1295 (La. Ct. App. 1993) (Wrongful adoption claim was brought before court, but was not addressed as the claim was dismissed because the one year prescription period for the claim had run).
Maine	"1. Information to be collected. The licensed child placing agency shall obtain medical and genetic in-	*Leroy v. Maine Children's Home*, 2002 WL 31360598 (Me. Super. 2002).

State	Statute	Case
	formation on the birth parents and the child... 2. Disclosure before placement. Prior to the child being placed for the purpose of adoption, the licensed child placing agency shall provide the information described in subsection 1 to the prospective adoptive parents." ME. REV. STAT. ANN. tit. 22 § 8205 (2011).	
Maryland	"A local department shall make reasonable efforts to compile and make available to a prospective adoptive parent: (1) all of the prospective adoptee's medical and mental health records that the local department has; or (2) a comprehensive medical and mental history of the prospective adoptee."	No

State	Statute	Case
	MD. CODE ANN., FAM. LAW § 5–356(a) (2012).	
Massachusetts	"The Department [of Social Services] shall provide the adoptive parent with all relevant information about a child to enable the adoptive parent to knowledgeably determine whether to accept the child for adoption." 110 MASS. CODE REGS. 7.213(3) (2012).	*Mohr v. Commonwealth*, 653 N.E.2d 1104, 1111 (Mass. 1995).
Michigan	"(1) Before placement of a child for adoption, a parent or guardian, a child placing agency, the department, or the court that places the child shall compile and provide to the prospective adoptive parent a written document containing all of the following non-identifying information ... (b) An account of the health and genetic	*Dresser v. Cradle of Hope Adoption Ctr., Inc.*, 358 F. Supp. 2d 620 (E.D. Mich. 2005).

State	Statute	Case
	history of the child."	
	MICH. COMP. LAWS § 710.27 (2012).	
Minnesota	"In any adoption under this chapter ... an agency, if an agency placement, shall provide a prospective adoptive parent with a complete, thorough, detailed, and current social and medical history of the child being adopted, if information is known after reasonable inquiry." MINN. STAT. § 259.43 (2012).	*M.H. and J.L.H. v. Caritas Family Services*, 488 N.W.2d 282 (Minn. 1992).
Mississippi	No	*Foster v. Bass*, 575 So.2d 967 (Miss. 1990) (Court proceeded on a negligence theory against the agency, and held that the disease in this case was too rare to be foreseeable and dismissed the claim).
Missouri	No	No

State	Statute	Case
Montana	"(1) Except for an adoption proceeding by a stepparent, in any adoption under this title, a birth parent, the department, or an agency shall provide a prospective adoptive parent with social and medical histories of the birth families, including tribal affiliation, if applicable." MONT. CODE ANN. § 42–3–101 (2011).	*Jackson v. State*, 956 P.2d 35 (Mont. 1998).
Nebraska	"A child placement agency, the department, or a private agency handling the adoption, as the case may be, shall maintain and shall provide to the adopting parents upon placement of the person with such parents and to the adopted person . . . the available medical history of the person placed for adoption and	No

State	Statute	Case
	of the biological parents''	
	NEB. REV. STAT. § 43–146.02 (2011).	
Nevada	"[T]he agency which provides child welfare services or a licensed child-placing agency shall provide the adopting parents of a child with a report which includes: (a) a copy of any medical records of the child which are in the possession of the agency, (b) any information obtained regarding: (1) the medical and sociological history of the child and the natural parents of the child." NEV. REV. STAT. §§ 127.152 (1)(a) and (b) (2011).	No
New Hampshire	No	No
New Jersey	No	No
New Mexico	No	No
New York	"[T]o the extent they are available, the medical histories of a child legally freed for	*Juman v. Louise Wise Services*, 620 N.Y.S.2d 371 (App. Div. 1995).

State	Statute	Case
	adoption or of a child to be placed in foster care and of his or her birth parents ... shall be provided by an authorized agency to such child's prospective adoptive parent." N.Y. Soc. Serv. Law § 373–a (McKinney 2010 & Supp. 2012).	
North Carolina	No	No
North Dakota	No	No
Ohio	"[T]he court promptly shall provide a copy of the social and medical histories [of the parents] filed with it to the petitioner." Ohio Rev. Code Ann. § 3107.09(E) (2011).	*Burr v. Board of County Com'rs of Stark County*, 491 N.E.2d 1101 (Ohio 1986).
Oklahoma	"[B]efore placing a minor for adoption, the Department of Human Services or a child-placing agency shall compile a written medical and social history report of the minor to be adopted."	No

State	Statute	Case
	OKLA. STAT. tit. 10, §§ 7504–1.1(A)(1) (2012).	
Oregon	"Before any judgment of adoption of a minor is entered, the court shall be provided a medical history of the child and of the biological parents as complete as possible under the circumstances." OR. REV. STAT. § 109.342 (1) (2012).	No
Pennsylvania	"(a) Filing places.—A statement regarding medical and social history information may be filed with the following: (1) The court that terminated parental rights. (2) The court that finalized the adoption. (3) The agency that coordinated the adoption. (4) The information registry established under Subchapter C (re-	*Gibbs v. Ernst*, 647 A.2d 882 (Pa. 1994).

State	Statute	Case
	lating to information registry)." 23 PA. CONS. STAT. ANN. § 2934 (2011).	
Rhode Island	No	*Mallette v. Children's Friend Service*, 661 A.2d 67 (R.I. 1995) (Court held that common-law negligent misrepresentation would be applied in the context of an adoption).
South Carolina	"(1) Before the placement of any child by any agency or by any person with a prospective adoptive parent, a preplacement investigation, a background investigation, and reports of these investigations must be completed: (c) a background information investigation and a report of this investigation may not disclose the identity of the biological parents of the	No

State	Statute	Case
	adoptee and shall provide the following: (i) a medical history of the biological family of the adoptee, including parents, siblings, and other family members related to the adoptee including ages, sex, race, and any known genetic, psychological, metabolic, or familial disorders; and (ii) a medical and developmental history of the adoptee." S.C. CODE ANN. §§ 63–9–520(1)(c)(i) and (ii) (2011).	
South Dakota	"[A]n adoptee or the adoptee's legal guardian having knowledge of a hospital or clinic with medical information of an adoptee's birth parent may provide a written request to the hospital or clinic for that information."	No

State	Statute	Case
	S.D. CODIFIED LAWS § 25–6–22 (2011).	
Tennessee	"Any person who, upon request by any party to an adoption . . . knowingly and willfully with-holds any infor-mation related to the child . . . or who knowingly and willfully with-holds any materi-al information concerning the identity, status, or whereabouts of the child's par-ents . . . commits a class A misde-meanor." TENN. CODE. ANN. § 36–1–104 (2012).	No
Texas	"Before placing a child for adoption, the Department of Protective and Regulatory Ser-vices, a licensed child-placing agency, or the child's parent or guardian shall compile a report on the available health, social, ed-ucational, and ge-	No

State	Statute	Case
	netic history of the child to be adopted''	
	TEX. FAM. CODE ANN. § 162.005 (b) (2011).	
Utah	''Upon finaliza-tion of an adop-tion in this state, the person who proceeded on be-half of the peti-tioner for adop-tion, or a child-placing agency if an agency is in-volved in the adoption, shall file a report with the office, in the form established by the office. That report shall in-clude a detailed health history, and a genetic and social history of the adoptee.''	No
	UTAH CODE ANN. § 78B–6–143 (1) (2008), *amended by*, 2012 Utah Laws S.B. 55 (West's No. 334).	
Vermont	''Before placing a minor for adop-tion, a parent or agency . . . shall provide in writing	No

State	Statute	Case
	to the prospective adoptive parent all of the following nonidentifying information . . . a social and health history of the minor." VT. STAT. ANN. tit 15a, § 2–105 (2012).	
Virginia	No	*Harshaw v. Bethany Christian Services*, 714 F. Supp. 2d 771 (W.D. Mich. 2010) (Court applied Virginia common law, and ruled that agency had the duty to obtain and disclose medical records of the adoptive child to the prospective adoptive parents).
Washington	"[T]he agency . . . shall transmit to the prospective adopting parent prior to placement . . . a complete medical report containing all known and available information concerning the mental, physi-	*McKinney v. State*, 950 P.2d 461 (Wash. 1998).

State	Statute	Case
	cal, and sensory handicaps of the child." WASH. REV. CODE § 26.33.350 (2011).	
West Virginia	"Whenever a person delivers a child for adoption the person first receiving such child and the prospective adopting parent or parents shall be entitled to receive from such person a written recital of all known circumstances surrounding the birth, medical and family medical history of the child, and an itemization of any facts or circumstances unknown concerning the child's parentage or that may require further development in the form of an affidavit from the birth mother consistent with the provisions of section 22–502."	*Wolford v. Children's Home Society of West Virginia*, 17 F.Supp.2d 577 (S.D. W. Va. 1998).

State	Statute	Case
	W. Va. Code § 48–22–401 (2012).	
Wisconsin	No	*Meracle v. Children's Service Society of Wisconsin*, 437 N.W.2d 532 (Wis. 1989).
Wyoming	"To the extent available, the medical history of a child subject to adoption and his natural parents, with information identifying the natural parents eliminated, shall be provided by an authorized agency or may be provided by order of a court to the child's adoptive parent any time after the adoption decree or to the child after he attains the age of majority." Wyo. Stat. Ann. § 1–22–116 (2011).	No

C. Expenses and Benefits of Adoption

The financial aspects of adoption vary depending on whether the adoption was private or accomplished through an agency. A private financial arrangement can be made between the birth parent and the adoptive parents, for example regarding medical insurance. If the birth mother has her own health insurance, the adoptive parents may be relieved of that expense. On the other hand, the adoptive parents may have to pay for the costs of the birth if the birth mother has no insurance. It is not unusual for the adoptive parents to support the birth mother during her pregnancy by providing living expenses. Agencies often have a fixed fee scale for the adoption process, making the cost of adoption predictable. Ordinarily, the financial aspects of adoption, whether the adoption is achieved by way of a private or agency placement, are scrutinized by courts to make sure that the process is not profit-making.

It should be noted that The Federal Adoption Tax Credit provides a tax credit for the costs of adoption like court costs and attorneys' fees so long as the adoption is not a step-parent adoption and the adopted child is a United States resident at the time of the adoption being finalized. Whether the tax credit will continue after 2011 is unclear. A limited number of states offer a state tax credit.

Some employers provide financial benefits to their employees who adopt children. Often these benefits include part of the cost of the adoption as well as paid parental leave. Further, adopted children are included in health insurance plans. The U. S. Military also provides benefits for active duty personnel who adopt children.

D. Consent of Birth Parents and Child

1. Mother's Consent

All state statutes require that the birth mother consent to the adoption of her child. No state allows consent before birth. States vary as to when consent can be given after the child has been born. The time frame may be twenty-four to forty-eight hours after birth, or three to ten days after birth depending on the state statute. At least four jurisdictions mandate psychological counseling or a social worker's examination before giving consent. Revocation of consent after placement is possible for statutory reasons like fraud, duress or undue influence. But the revocation must occur within a certain time frame like three, ten, fifteen, thirty, forty-five or sixty days after execution of the relinquishment. However, there are statutory requirements as to the reason for the revocation. Some states require that the revocation be in the child's best interests.

a. Adoption Consent Statutes

State	Citation[1]	Waiting Period Before Adoption Allowed	Time for Withdrawal of Consent	Age at which Child's Consent Needed
Alabama	ALA. CODE §§ 26–10A–7, 26–10A–13, 26–10A–14 (2012).	Allowed at birth.	5 days after petition or 5 days after birth; or 14 days if determined by court to be reasonable	14 years.

State	Citation[1]	Waiting Period Before Adoption Allowed	Time for Withdrawal of Consent	Age at which Child's Consent Needed
			and in best interests of child.	
Alaska	ALASKA STAT. §§ 25.23.040, 25.23.070 (2012).	Allowed at birth.	10 days after petition or anytime if in best interests of child.	10 years unless court orders adoption without consent.
Arizona	ARIZ. REV. STAT. §§ 8–106 to 107 (2012).	72 hours.	Consent irrevocable.	12 years, must be given in open court.
Arkansas	ARK. CODE ANN. §§ 9–9–206, 208 to 209 (2011).	Allowed at birth.	10 days unless waived, in which case 5 days after signature or birth; irrevocable upon issuance of adoption decree.	12 years unless court orders adoption without consent.
California	CAL. FAM. CODE §§ 8602, 8700, 8801.3, 8814.5 (2012).	Allowed at birth, though counseling required at least 10 days prior to giving consent.	Independent adoption: revocable for 30 days; agency adoption: revocable for 10 days, unless adoptive family specified and placement fails, in which case revocable for 30 days.	12 years.
Colorado	COLO. REV. STAT. §§ 19–5–103(1)(a), 19–5–104(7)(a), 19–5–203(2)	Allowed at birth, though counseling required prior to re-	90 days, but only on proof of fraud or duress.	12 years.

State	Citation[1]	Waiting Period Before Adoption Allowed	Time for Withdrawal of Consent	Age at which Child's Consent Needed
	(2012).	linquish-ment pro-ceeding.		
Connecticut	CONN. GEN. STAT. §§ 45a–715(d), 45a–715(j), 45a–727(c)(1) (2012).	48 hours.	Consent ir-revocable.	12 years.
Delaware	DEL. CODE ANN. tit. 13, §§ 907, 909 (2011).	Allowed at birth.	60 days, subject to court ap-proval.	14 years, unless court orders adop-tion without consent.
District of Columbia	D.C. CODE § 16–304, 310 (2012).	Not speci-fied statuto-rily.	Up to one year for a procedural or jurisdic-tional de-fect.	14 years
Florida	FLA. STAT. §§ 63.062, 63.082 (2012).	48 hours, or release from hospital, whichever is earlier.	3 business days.	12 years, unless court orders adop-tion without consent.
Georgia	GA. CODE ANN. §§ 19–8–4, 19–8–9 (2011).	Allowed at birth.	10 days, un-less last day would be a Saturday, Sunday, or legal holi-day, in which case next busi-ness day.	14 years.
Hawaii	HAW. REV. STAT. §§ 578–1.5, 578–2 (2011).	Allowed at birth.	Irrevocable without court order showing withdrawal would be in best inter-est of child.	10 years, unless court orders adop-tion without consent.
Idaho	IDAHO CODE ANN. §§ 16–1504, 16–	Allowed at birth.	Upon peti-tion and court order,	12 years, unless child lacks men-

State	Citation[1]	Waiting Period Before Adoption Allowed	Time for Withdrawal of Consent	Age at which Child's Consent Needed
	1515 (2012).		but revoking parents must compensate prospective adoptive parents for expenses.	tal capacity.
Illinois	750 ILL. COMP. STAT. 50/9; 50/11—12 (2011).	72 hours.	Irrevocable except on proof of fraud or duress; pre-birth consent of a father revocable for 72 hours after birth.	14 years, consent may be waived if child needs mental treatment or is mentally handicapped.
Indiana	IND. CODE §§ 31–19–9–1 to 31–19–10–4 (2011).	Allowed at birth.	30 days, but not after issuance of decree, and only if in best interests of child.	14 years.
Iowa	IOWA CODE §§ 600.7, 600A.4 (2012).	72 hours.	Anytime prior to issuance of decree for adoptive parents; custody release automatically revocable for 96 hours after signing, or upon showing of good cause later.	14 years.
Kansas	KAN. STAT. ANN. §§ 59–2114, 2129 (2012).	12 hours.	Consent irrevocable except on proof that not freely	14 years if of "sound intellect."

State	Citation[1]	Waiting Period Before Adoption Allowed	Time for Withdrawal of Consent	Age at which Child's Consent Needed
			and voluntarily given.	
Kentucky	KY. REV. STAT. ANN. § 199.500 (2011).	72 hours.	20 days after consent and placement approval, whichever is later.	12 years, unless court orders adoption without consent.
Louisiana	LA. CHILD. CODE ANN. art. 1122—1123, 1130, 1195 (2011).	For mother: 3 days for agency adoption, and 5 days for private adoption; for father: can do earlier than 5 days for either agency or private adoption.	Consent irrevocable unless their is fraud or duress, but legitimate father's prebirth consent not irrevocable until 5 days after birth.	Child's consent not required.
Maine	ME. REV. STAT. ANN. tit. 18–A, §§ 9–202, 9–302 (2011).	Allowed at birth, though petition must be pending.	3 days.	14 years.
Maryland	MD. CODE ANN., FAM. LAW §§ 5–338—339, 5–3B–21(2) (2012).	Allowed at birth.	30 days after signing or filing of petition, whichever is later. If consent is entered before a judge, then the time for withdrawing consent is waived.	Child must be represented by an attorney, and, if over 10, consents, or, if under 10, does not object.
Massachusetts	MASS. GEN. LAWS ch. 210, § 2 (2012).	4 days.	Consent irrevocable.	12 years.
Michigan	MICH. COMP. LAWS §§ 710.29,	Allowed at birth, though ad-	Anytime prior to placement	14 years.

State	Citation[1]	Waiting Period Before Adoption Allowed	Time for Withdrawal of Consent	Age at which Child's Consent Needed
	710.31, 710.43, 710.44 (2012).	judication of putative father's rights and judicial explanation of consequences required prior to consent.	for adoption, but only by court order after hearing.	
Minnesota	MINN. STAT. §§ 259.24 (2a), 259.24(3), 259.24 (6a) (2012).	72 hours.	10 days, or later upon proof that consent was obtained by fraud.	14 years.
Mississippi	MISS. CODE ANN. §§ 93–17–5, 93–17–15 (2010).	72 hours.	Consent irrevocable, but parents may bring an action to set aside adoption decree within 6 months.	14 years.
Missouri	MO. REV. STAT. § 453.030 (2011).	48 hours.	Anytime until reviewed and accepted by judge.	14 years, unless court finds child lacks mental capacity.
Montana	MONT. CODE ANN. §§ 42–2–301, 42–2–408, 42–2–410 (2011).	72 hours, and counseling required prior to giving consent.	Anytime prior to issuance of order, but only by mutual agreement with adoptive parents.	12 years, unless child lacks mental capacity.
Nebraska	NEB. REV. STAT. § 43–104 (2011) *invalidated by In re Adoption of Corbin J.*, 775 N.W.2d 404 (Neb. 2009)	48 hours.	Consent irrevocable.	14 years.

State	Citation[1]	Waiting Period Before Adoption Allowed	Time for Withdrawal of Consent	Age at which Child's Consent Needed
	([S]tatutes allowing adoption of child to proceed without putative biological father's consent were unconstitutional as applied to putative biological father, who had established a familial relationship with child).			
Nevada	Nev. Rev. Stat. §§ 127.020, 127.070 (2011).	72 hours.	Mother's consent irrevocable unless adoptive parents found unsuitable; prior consent from unwed father invalidated upon marriage to mother, 6 months without consent from mother, or 2 years without a petition.	14 years.
New Hampshire	N.H. REV. STAT. ANN. §§ 170–B:3, 170–B:8, 170–B:12 (2011).	72 hours.	Anytime prior to entry of final decree, but only (1) on proof of	14 years, unless court orders adoption without consent in best inter-

State	Citation[1]	Waiting Period Before Adoption Allowed	Time for Withdrawal of Consent	Age at which Child's Consent Needed
			fraud or duress; *or* (2) if in best interests of child.	ests of child.
New Jersey	N.J. STAT. §§ 9:3–41 (a), 9:3–41(e), 9:3–49 (2012).	72 hours.	Consent irrevocable except by agency discretion or court order showing fraud or duress.	10 years, if child can form intelligent preference, court shall give consideration, unless waived for good cause.
New Mexico	N.M. STAT. §§ 32A–5–17, 32A–5–21 (G), 32A–5–21 (I) (2011).	48 hours.	Consent irrevocable, except before decree of adoption on proof of fraud or duress.	14 years, unless child lacks mental capacity.
New York	N.Y. DOM. REL. LAW §§ 111, 115–b (2011).	Allowed at birth.	Judicial consent irrevocable; non-judicial consent revocable for 45 days, though adoptive parents may dispute revocation, in which case, court will make determination according to best interest of the child.	14 years, unless court orders adoption without consent.
North Carolina	N.C. GEN. STAT. §§ 48–3–601, 48–3–603 to 48–3–	Mother's consent allowed at birth; fa-	Generally irrevocable, but pre-birth con-	12 years, unless court orders adoption without

State	Citation[1]	Waiting Period Before Adoption Allowed	Time for Withdrawal of Consent	Age at which Child's Consent Needed
	604, 48–3–607 to 48–3–609 (2011).	ther's allowed anytime, including before birth.	sent revocable for 7 days, or by proof of fraud or duress, or by mutual agreement with adoptive parents.	consent in best interests of child.
North Dakota	N.D. Cent. Code §§ 14–15–05, 14–15–07 to 14–15–08 (2011).	Allowed at birth.	Any time prior to entry of a decree if in best interests of child.	10 years, unless court orders adoption without consent in best interests of child.
Ohio	Ohio Rev. Code §§ 3107.06—3107.07, 3107.08(A), 3107.084 (2011).	72 hours.	Revocable until interlocutory or final order if in best interests of child.	12 years, unless court orders adoption without consent in best interests of child.
Oklahoma	Okla. Stat. tit. 10, §§ 7503–2.1 to 7503–2.3, 7503–2.6 to 7503–2.7 (2012).	Mother's consent allowed at birth; putative father's consent allowed anytime, including before birth; legitimate father's consent allowed at birth.	Judicial consent revocable if no petition filed for 9 months, or if another required consent not executed, or if obtained by fraud or duress; nonjudicial consent revocable for 15 days.	12 years, unless court orders adoption with consent.
Oregon	Or. Rev. Stat. §§ 109.312, 109.328 (2012).	Allowed at birth.	Consent may be given together with a certificate of irrevocability,	14 years.

State	Citation[1]	Waiting Period Before Adoption Allowed	Time for Withdrawal of Consent	Age at which Child's Consent Needed
			thereafter revocable only on proof of fraud or duress.	
Pennsylvania	23 PA. CONS. STAT. ANN. § 2711 (2011).	Mother's consent allowed after 72 hours; putative father's consent allowed at birth.	30 days after execution; or by proof of fraud or duress 60 days after birth or execution, but not more than 30 days after entry of decree.	12 years.
Rhode Island	R.I. GEN. LAWS §§ 15– 7–5, 15–7–6, 15–7–21.1 (2011).	15 days.	180 days after entry of decree if in best interests of child.	14 years.
South Carolina	S.C. CODE §§ 63–9–310, 63–9–330, 63–9– 350(2012).	Allowed at birth.	Before decree if in best interests of child and on proof that consent was obtained by duress or coercion.	14 years unless child lacks mental capacity or requiring consent is not in best interests of child.
South Dakota	S.D. CODIFIED LAWS §§ 25– 5A–4, 25–6– 5, 25–6–21 (2012).	5 days.	Consent irrevocable, except for fraud, though claims regarding rights to child may be brought for 2 years.	12 years.
Tennessee	TENN. CODE ANN. §§ 36–	3 days, though	Anytime before entry of	14 years, or, if mentally

State	Citation[1]	Waiting Period Before Adoption Allowed	Time for Withdrawal of Consent	Age at which Child's Consent Needed
	1–111 to 36–1–112, 36–1–117 (2012).	court may waive waiting period for good cause.	order for parental consent, else 10 days; or within 30 days of order for proof of fraud or duress.	disabled, by a guardian ad litem.
Texas	TEX. FAM. CODE §§ 161.103, 161.106, 162.010 (2011).	Mother's consent allowed after 48 hours; a man may consent anytime, including before birth.	Putative father's consent revocable before order; otherwise revocability may be specified by contract, where unspecified, revocable for 11 days.	12 years, unless court orders adoption without consent in best interests of child.
Utah	UTAH CODE §§ 78B–6–120 to 121, 125 to 126 (2011).	Mother's consent allowed after 24 hours; all others may consent anytime, including before birth.	Consent irrevocable.	12 years, unless child lacks capacity.
Vermont	VT. STAT. ANN. tit. 15A, §§ 2–401, 2–404, 2–407 to 2–409 (2012).	36 hours.	21 days.	14 years, unless court orders adoption without consent.
Virginia	VA. CODE ANN. §§ 63.2–1202, 63.2–1204, 63.2–1223, 63.2–1234 (2011).	72 hours, though putative father may execute pre-birth consent.	When child reaches age of 10 days and 7 days have elapsed since execution of agreement.	14 years, unless court orders adoption without consent in best interests of child.

State	Citation[1]	Waiting Period Before Adoption Allowed	Time for Withdrawal of Consent	Age at which Child's Consent Needed
Washington	WASH. REV. CODE §§ 26.33.080, 26.33.160 (2012).	Allowed at anytime, including before birth, though 48 hours after birth required before presentation to court.	Anytime prior to court approval, if received within 48 hours of approval.	14 years.
West Virginia	W. VA. CODE §§ 48–22–301 to 48–22–303, 48–22–305 (2012).	72 hours.	Revocation allowed by contract, or by mutual agreement with adoptive parents, or on proof or fraud or duress.	12 years, unless court orders adoption without consent.
Wisconsin	WIS. STAT. §§ 48.42, 48.46(2), 48.837 (2011).	Allowed at birth.	Consent irrevocable except on proof of impropriety, including fraud, mistake, or new evidence.	Child given notice at 12 years.
Wyoming	WYO. STAT. ANN. §§ 1–22–109, 1–22–109(d) (2011).	Allowed at birth.	Consent irrevocable except on proof of fraud or duress, or if adoption denied because putative father does not consent, mother may withdraw consent.	14 years.

[1] Parenthetical dates indicate the year of the last legislative session through which the citation provided is current.

2. Standby Adoption

Iowa and Illinois have authorized standby adoption, which in Iowa's statute is "an adoption in which a terminally ill parent consents to termination of parental rights and the issuance of a final adoption decree effective upon the occurrence of a future event, which is either the death of the terminally ill parent or the request of the parent for the issuance of a final adoption decree." Iowa Code Ann. § 600.14A (West 2011). The provisions regarding standby adoption in Illinois can be found in 750 Ill. Comp. Stat. Ann. §§ 50/13(D); 50/13.1. The procedures to be followed for a standby adoption can be found in Administrative Order 2008–8 (Circuit Court of Cook County, Illinois, County Department, County Division) issued by Presiding Judge Patrick McGann, July 3, 2008.

3. Waiver of Consent

If a court determines that the mother's consent to the adoption of her child should be waived because of the mother's abandonment of her child or her unfitness or her neglecting of the child for example, the judge ordinarily has the statutory authority to order the waiver. Waiver of consent is often an issue in an involuntary termination of parental rights case, not in the situation of the direct placement of the child by the child's birth mother, and if the waiver of consent is supported by convincing evidence, the result is the child's adoption.

4. Child's Consent

State statutes generally set the age of ten to fourteen for the consent of a child for her adoption. This age requirement reflects a concern for taking into account the child's wishes. Requiring the pre-adolescent and adolescent child's consent also means that such a child can prevent his or her own adoption, which might be the case if the child wishes to remain with foster parents or does not want to be adopted by a step-parent. Unless the state statute makes the age at which a child must consent mandatory, like the Georgia statute, which provides that a child fourteen years old or older must consent in writing (GA. CODE ANN. § 19–7–5(b), judges may be able to override the child's wishes whether unconditionally or with a determination that the adoption would advance the child's welfare.

5. Father's Consent

Before the 1970s, the birth father's role in the adoption process was, for the most part, minimal. The reason was both historical and practical. Historically, under the early common law, a child born out of wedlock was considered the child of no one, *fillius nullius*, only later to be considered the child of her mother. That status had legal consequences. Fathers of illegitimate children had no rights (for example, custodial or inheritance) to them and such children had no rights (like inheritance) against their fathers. Those fathers were treated as shadow figures, both in society and in law. Unless the father's identity was legally established and his whereabouts known, his consent to the adoption of his child was not necessary.

That changed with the 1972 United States Supreme Court's decision in *Stanley v. Illinois*, 405 U.S. 645 (1972). In that case, Peter Stanley had lived with the mother of his three children off and on for eighteen years when Joan Stanley died. Peter and Joan had never married and consequently upon her death, according to Illinois law, the state instituted a dependency proceeding which resulted in the three children becoming wards of the State. They were removed from the custody of their father and were placed with court-appointed guardians. Mr. Stanley appealed the decision, claiming that his children had been removed from his custody without his having been shown to be unfit. By such action, he argued, he was being treated differently from married fathers resulting in his being denied equal protection of the law guaranteed him by the Fourteenth Amendment to the U. S. Constitution. The Illinois Supreme Court acknowledged that Mr. Stanley's unfitness had not been established, but rejected the equal protection claim, holding that Mr. Stanley's status as an unwed father was the critical factor, not his fitness for fatherhood, and affirmed the removal.

The United States Supreme Court saw Mr. Stanley's plight differently. To the Court, the State of

Illinois' presumption that unwed fathers, merely by the fact that they had not married the mother of their children, were unfit could not stand. Unwed fathers, the Court held, are parents and as parents are constitutionally entitled to a hearing on their fitness before their children are removed from their custody. The Court further held that the denial of such a hearing violates the equal protection clause.

Stanley v. Illinois was a dependency hearing case, not an adoption case, yet the Court referred to the adoption proceeding in a footnote that has become famous. Footnote 9 reads:

> We note in passing that the incremental cost of offering unwed fathers an opportunity for individualized hearings on fitness, appears to be minimal. If unwed fathers, in the main, do not care about the disposition of their children, they will not appear to demand hearings. If they do care, under the scheme here held invalid, Illinois would admittedly at some later time have to afford them a properly focused hearing in a custody or adoption proceeding.
>
> Extending opportunity for hearing to unwed fathers who desire and claim competence to care for their children creates no constitutional or procedural obstacle to foreclosing those unwed fathers who are not so included.

405 U.S. 645, 657 (1972). With that footnote, the United States Supreme Court put in question every state adoption statute in the United States at that time. Fathers of illegitimate children could no long-

er be ignored in the adoption process. Nor could children be relinquished for adoption, either directly by their birth mother or through a licensed adoption agency, without recognizing that the birth father had rights to be heard in the adoption proceeding unless his consent to the adoption had been properly obtained or waived.

Left unanswered by footnote 9, and the remainder of the *Stanley* decision, was the notice due to a putative father when his child was relinquished for adoption and an adoption proceeding commenced. Notifying the father, of course, requires knowledge concerning the father's identity. If the birth mother is unable to identify the father, how can the U. S. Supreme Court's mandate be implemented? Section 24 of The Uniform Parentage Act required service by publication or posting where the court determines that such service would be likely to lead to the identification of the father. Section 3 of The Uniform Putative and Unknown Fathers Act also requires notice to "every putative father of the child known [to the person the person seeking termination]": (a) "at a time and place and in a manner appropriate under the [rules of civil procedure for the service of process in a civil action] or (ii) at a time and place and in a manner as the court directs and which provides actual notice."

As a response to the requirement of notice set out in *Stanley*, some states have enacted laws that establish Putative Father Registries. Under those laws, notice must be given to men who register as fathers of particular children. Whether putative fathers know about the Registry or not, unless they register, for example by mailing a postcard to the registry as per New York law, their right to notice is jeopardized. Such was the holding in *Lehr v. Robertson*, 463 U.S. 248 (1983), decided eleven years after *Stanley* and which determined that the Putative Father Registry in New York did not violate the Due Process Clause of the U. S. Constitution.

To Justice John Paul Sevens, who wrote the majority opinion in *Lehr*, a birth father must have more than a biological connection with his child to trigger constitutional protections of notice and an opportunity to be heard in an adoption proceeding. The putative father must have assumed a significant parental role in the child's life. Justice Stevens wrote:

> The significance of the biological connection is that it offers the natural father an opportunity that no other male possesses to develop a relationship with his offspring. If he grasps that opportunity and accepts some measure of respectability for the child's future, he may enjoy the blessings of the parent-child relationship and make uniquely valuable contribution to the child's development. If he fails to do so, the Federal Constitution will not automatically compel a State to listen to his opinion of where the child's best interests lie."

Lehr v. Robertson, 463 U.S. 248 (1983). *Lehr* followed *Quilloin v. Walcott*, 434 U.S. 246 (1978),

which held that an unwed father's due process and
equal protection rights were not violated by a Georgia statute that only required the consent of the
birth mother and not the consent of the putative
father if he did not comply with its legitimation
procedures. In that case, the birth mother had
married and the child's step-father wished to adopt
the child over the birth father's objection. Where
the birth father failed to provide financial support
and was uninvolved with his child's upbringing, he
was not entitled to due process protections before
his child was adopted. The result of the case was to
recognize the *de facto* family unit that had been
established by the child's mother and her husband.

Yet, where a biological father establishes a relationship with his children, that relationship does
give rise to constitutional protection. In *Caban v.
Mohammed*, 441 U.S. 380 (1979), decided by the U.
S. Supreme Court a year after *Quilloin*, the biological father's two illegitimate children were adopted
by the husband of their birth mother. The birth
father did not consent. Nor was his consent required by New York law, which permitted adoption
of an illegitimate child upon the consent of the birth
mother. The issue in *Caban* was whether the New
York statute violated a putative father's rights under the Equal Protection Clause of the Fourteenth
Amendment because it treated unwed fathers differently from unwed mothers on the assumption that
"a natural mother, absent special circumstances,
bears a closer relationship with her child than a
father does." In *Caban*, the children's birth father

supported them for a time, developed a relationship with them through visits, and had temporary custody (although the custody was in violation of an agreement with the children's mother). The Court, reversed the decision of the New York Court of Appeals and held that lumping all putative fathers together, those who maintain a relationship with their children and those who do not, is an "overbroad generalization." In Justice Stevens' dissent, he clarified the decision as he saw it by restricting the holding to the adoption of older children who have had a substantial relationship with their birth fathers. That idea was reinforced four years later in his decision in *Lehr* and his statement about putative fathers "grasping the opportunity" for fatherhood in order to assert their rights in an adoption proceeding.

a. Putative Father Registry

State	Statute	Details
Alabama	ALA. CODE § 26–10C–1 (2012).	Alabama Putative Father Registry Office of Adoption Department of Human Resources 50 N. Ripley Street Montgomery, AL 36130–4000
Alaska	ALASKA STAT. § 25.27.165 (2012).	No registry.
Arizona	ARIZ. REV. STAT.	Arizona Dept. of

State	Statute	Details
	Ann. § 8–106.01 (2012)	Health Services PO Box 3887 Phoenix, AZ 85030 ($5.00 fee to search; No fee to file)
Arkansas	Ark. Code Ann. § 20–18–702 (2011).	Legal Section/Vital Records 4815 W. Markham Street Little Rock, AR 72205–3867 ($5.00 fee)
California	Ca. Fam. Code § 7571 (2012).	No registry. However, the putative father must bring an action declaring existence of a father child relationship within 30 days of being presented with notice of an adoption proceeding.
Colorado	Colo. Rev. Stat. §§ 19–1–301 to 312(2012).	No registry. However, a putative father must file an act of paternity within 30 days of birth or of receiving notice that he may be likely father. The putative father must file an answer within 20

State	Statute	Details
		days after service of notice of termination.
Connecticut	CONN. GEN. STAT. §§ 45a–743 to 762 (2012).	No registry. The putative father can assert paternity at any time, but not later than 60 days of notice of termination of parental rights.
Delaware	DEL. CODE ANN. tit. 13, § 8–402 (2011).	Provides for father to file in the "Registry of Paternity". Division of Child Support Enforcement P.O. Box 904 84A Christiana Road New Castle, DE 19720
District of Columbia	D.C. CODE §§ 16–301 to 316 (2012).	No registry.
Florida	FLA. STAT. § 63.054 (2012).	Florida Dept. of Health Office of Vital Statistics PO Box 210 Jacksonville, FL 32231–0049 ($9.00 fee & filing requires a specific form)
Georgia	GA. CODE ANN. § 19–11–9 (2011).	Vital Records 2600 Skyland Drive NE

State	Statute	Details
		Atlanta, GA 30319 ($10 fee)
Hawaii	HAW. REV. STAT. §§ 578–1 to 17 (2011).	No registry.
Idaho	IDAHO CODE ANN. § 16–1513 (2012).	Vital Statistics Unit PO Box 83720 Boise, ID 83720–0036
Illinois	750 ILL. COMP. STAT. 50/12.1 (2011).	Illinois Putative Father Registry 3 N Old State Capitol Plaza Springfield IL 62701 www.putative father.org ($40 fee required, which includes online search access)
Indiana	IND. CODE § 31–19–5–12 (2011).	Indiana State Department of Health 2 North Meridian Street Indianapolis, IN 46204
Iowa	IOWA CODE §§ 144.12A & 600A.6 (2012).	Vital Records Bureau, Lucas Building 321 East 12th Street Des Moines, IA, 50319–0075
Kansas	KAN. STAT. ANN. §§ 59–2111 to 2144 (2012).	Kansas Dept. of Social & Rehab Services PO Box 497

State	Statute	Details
		Topeka, KS 66601–0497
Kentucky	KY. REV. STAT. ANN. §§ 199.470 to .590 (2011).	No registry.
Louisiana	LA. REV. STAT. Ann. § 9:400 (2011).	Vital Records PO Box 60630 New Orleans, LA 70160–0630
Maine	ME. REV. STAT. ANN. tit. 22, § 2706–A (2011).	No registry. However, a putative father has 20 days after notice of adoption proceeding to file a claim.
Maryland	MD. CODE ANN., FAM. LAW §§ 5–4C–01 to–07 (2012).	No registry.
Massachusetts	MASS. GEN. LAWS ch. 210 § 4A (2012).	This is not a true registry, but provides for a parental claim form. Office of General Counsel Department of Social Services 24 Farnsworth Street Boston MA 02210
Michigan	MICH. COMP. LAWS § 710.33 (2012)	File a form called the "notice of intent to claim paternity" (DCH 7038) with the Central Father Registry. Central Father Registry Michi-

State	Statute	Details
		gan Dept. of Community Health Vital Records, Health Statistics 3423 N. Martin Luther King Boulevard Lansing, MI 48906 ($10.00 filing fee)
Minnesota	MINN. STAT. § 259.52 (2012).	Office of the State Registrar P.O. Box 64882 St. Paul, MN 55164–0882
Mississippi	MISS. CODE ANN. §§ 93–17–201 to 223 (2011).	No registry.
Missouri	MO. REV. STAT. § 192.016 (2011).	Missouri Dept. of Health; Senior Services Bureau of Vital Records PO Box 570 Jefferson City. MO 65102–0570
Montana	MONT. CODE ANN. § 42–2–202 (2011).	Bureau of Vital Statistics 111 N. Sanders, Room 205 Helena, MT 59620 ($10.00 fee)
Nebraska	NEB. REV. STAT. §§ 43–104.01 & 02 (2011).	Nebraska Health & Human Services Vital Statistics Section P.O. Box 95065

State	Statute	Details
		Lincoln, NE 68509–5065
Nevada	NEV. REV. STAT. §§ 127.003 to .009 (2011).	No registry.
New Hampshire	N.H. REV. STAT. ANN §§ 170–B:1 to B:31 (2011).	Department of Health & Human Services Division of Child Support Services 129 Pleasant Street Concord, NH 03301
New Jersey	N.J. STAT. ANN. §§ 9:3–37 to–56 (2012).	No registry. However, under §§ 9:3–45 and 9:3–45.1, a written objection can be filed within 20 days of receipt of notice of termination.
New Mexico	N.M. STAT. ANN. § 32A–5–20 (2011).	Laura Gutierrez, Registration Supervisor Bureau of Vital Records/Health Services PO Box 26110 Santa Fe, NM 87502
New York	N.Y. SOC. SERV. LAW § 372–c (2011).	NYS OCF/PFR Capital View Office Park 52 Washington St., Room 323 No. Rensselaer, NY 12144–2796

State	Statute	Details
North Carolina	N.C. GEN. STAT. §§ 48–9–101 to 109 (2012).	No registry.
North Dakota	N.D. CENT. CODE §§ 14–15–01 to 23 (2011).	No registry.
Ohio	OHIO REV. CODE ANN. § 3107.062 (2011).	Ohio Dept. Job and Family Services P.O. Box 182709 Columbus, OH 43218–2709 (Specific form required for filing.)
Oklahoma	OKLA. STAT. ANN. tit. 10 § 7506–1.1 (2012).	Dept. of Human Services—Adoptions PO Box 25352 Oklahoma, City, OK 73125
Oregon	OR. REV. STAT. § 109.430 (2012).	A voluntary adoption registry provides the mechanism for putative fathers, birth parents and adult adoptees can agree to share information. Bureau of Vital Records PO Box 14050 Portland, OR 97923–0050
Pennsylvania	23 PA. CONS. STAT. ANN. §§ 2901—2910 (West 2011).	No registry, but inquiries may be made to: Bureau of Child Support Enforcement

State	Statute	Details
		ATTN: Paternity Services Coordinator Post Office Box 8018 Harrisburg PA 17105
Rhode Island	R.I. GEN. LAWS §§ 15–7.2–1 to 15 (2011).	No registry.
South Carolina	S.C. CODE ANN. §§ 20–7–1646 to 1897 (2012).	No registry.
South Dakota	S.D. CODIFIED LAWS §§ 25–6–1 to 25 (2012).	No registry.
Tennessee	TENN. CODE ANN. § 36–2–318 (2012).	Department of Children's Services Cordell Hull Building— 8th Floor 436 Sixth Avenue, North Nashville TN 37243
Texas	TEX. FAM. CODE ANN. § 160.401 (2011).	A paternity registry exists, and more information can be found at www.dshs. state.tx.us/ reqproc/forms. The putative father must file Form VS134. Dept. Of State Health Services P.O. Box 12040 Austin, TX 78711–2040

State	Statute	Details
		($10 filing fee)
Utah	UTAH CODE ANN. § 78B–6–121 (West 2011).	Bureau of Vital Records 288 North 1460 West PO Box 141012 Salt Lake City, UT 84114–1012
Vermont	VT. STAT. ANN. tit. 15A, §§ 6–101 to 112 (2012).	No registry.
Virginia	VA. CODE ANN. §§ 63.2–1249 to 1253 (2012).	The statute provides for an on-line registry with search functionality. Send inquiry emails to PutativeFather@dss.virginia.gov Department of Social Services 7 North Eighth St. Richmond VA 23219–3301
Washington	WASH. REV. CODE §§ 26.33.010 to .901 (2012).	No registry.
West Virginia	W. VA. CODE §§ 48–23–501 to 507 (2012).	No registry.
Wisconsin	WIS. STAT. §§ 48.40 to .435 (2012).	No registry.
Wyoming	WYO. STAT. ANN. §§ 1–22–117 (2011).	Department of Family Services Hathaway Building 3rd Floor Cheyenne, WY 82002

II.   Involuntary System

A.   Placement After Dependency Adjudication

More children are adopted through the child dependency process than are adopted by way of a birth mother's voluntary relinquishment. That process involves complex legal issues which include removal of the child from the birth mother's custody and placement with a public social service agency after a judicial hearing. To justify removal of a child from her birth parents, the agency must show, according to the United States Supreme Court case of *Santosky v. Kramer*, 455 U.S. 745 (1982), with at least clear and convincing evidence that the child has been neglected by her birth parents. Some states may require a higher standard of proof, a possibility the *Santosky* case left open, such as beyond a reasonable doubt, but ordinarily the standard is clear and convincing evidence. In addition to neglect, a child may be removed because of physical, emotional or sexual abuse, non-support and the parent's unfitness caused by drug addition, alcoholism or severe mental illness. The removal and subsequent placement with foster parents may be either temporary or permanent. It may occur after the agency has been unsuccessful in its efforts to rehabilitate the parent and assist her in meeting the needs of the child in the child's home

Ordinarily, if the child has been removed for the parent's custody, the agency under whose care the child has been placed by a judge enters into an agreement with the birth mother that provides for the conditions that must be met in order for the child to be reunited with her mother. The conditions vary depending on the reason for the removal. Conditions may include completion of a rehabilitation program to overcome dependency on alcohol or drugs, the obtaining of suitable housing, the achieving of independent living and employment, or the completing of some sort of parenting program. In addition, the agreement may set out a schedule for the birth mother to visit her child in foster care so that if there has been a positive bonding between birth parent and child, it will continue. In addition to abandonment, the most common ground for the termination of birth parents' rights is the failure of the birth parents, usually the mother, to fulfill the conditions for the return of her child from foster care coupled with a determination that termination is in the best interests of the child. There is no uniformity in state laws as to whether a permanent placement plan like adoption is necessary before a termination order is issued.

State statutory laws regulating the termination of parental rights as a separate court proceeding have been influenced by the proposals of the then United States Department of Health, Education & Welfare (now Department of Health & Human Services) during the 1960s and 1970s when Children's Bureau in that department was actively involved in developing model state laws that could facilitate the adoption of children.

The three major model acts that Children's Bureau proposed to states for their consideration were: Model Child Abuse Mandatory Reporting Act, Model Act to Free Children for Permanent Placement and the Model Subsidized Adoption Act. All three have had a profound effect on the adoption of children and changed the way child welfare services were offered.

Congress also was interested in child welfare reform and it passed the Child Abuse Prevention and Treatment and Adoption Reform Act of 1978 (42 U.S.C. § 5111). That act dealt with removing the barriers to adoption as well as supporting grants for child abuse and neglect prevention.

There were three basic reasons for Children's Bureau's interest in developing those three model acts. They were: (1) recognition of a large number of children who were in foster care for up to five years depending on the state, often unable to return home because of the inability of their parents to care for them properly or because they had been physically or emotionally abused; (2) the legal obstacles of terminating parental rights; and (3) the difficulties, especially financial, foster parents faced when they desired to adopt the children in their care.

During the 1960s, there was a noticeable increase in children who were seen in hospitals with unusual and sometimes inexplicable injuries, considered not to be accidental but intentionally inflicted by the child's parents or caretaker. Often, the parent's justification for the injury was that they had exercised their parental authority of punishing the child and were immune from any prosecution. The point of the mandatory reporting by pediatricians, nurses, teachers and others to an appropriate governmental authority was to prompt some kind of state intervention that would result in an investigation, ordinarily by a state child welfare agency. Physicians' reporting child abuse was thought to jeopardize the doctor-patient privilege. Because of that, some medical groups opposed the mandate. Ultimately, however physicians became convinced that a child's welfare trumped the privilege.

After a report of child abuse had been made to the proper authorities, the investigation that followed might lead to allowing the child to remain in the custody of his parents with supervision by a social worker, removal of the child and placement in temporary foster care, or if the injuries were severe and the child would be in imminent danger of further abuse, the child could be placed in permanent foster care, possibly resulting in the termination of parental rights and ultimately adoption.

Termination of parental rights is an enormously serious act. It flies in the face of history, law and tradition in the United States, where parents are the primary caretakers for their children and have the legal responsibility of raising them without state intervention. It has been said time and time again in legal decisions that parents have a liberty interest in their children. On the other hand, the state historically has a duty to protect children from harm during their minority under the doctrine of *parens patriae*. A balance has to be achieved between a parent's responsibility and the state's duty.

During the 1960s and 1970s, mental health specialists advanced the idea that from infancy to adolescence, children needed to feel secure, safe and wanted by their nurturing parents who were the children's primary caretakers. They also proposed that one of the major factors in a child's healthy development was a child's attachment to an adult figure like the child's parent, who has a continuous relationship with the child. To mental health and child development specialists, continuity of care was critical. Removal of a child from her parents and placement with foster parents was considered a serious blow to a child's healthy psychological development, even when on balance the removal was in the child's best interests. Additionally, a child's placement with a series of foster parents was believed to have a detrimental impact on a child's emotional development because it involved multiple separations and attachments with parental figures as well as interruptions in the child's educational advancement. It was therefore thought important for law-makers to emphasize the positive goal of permanence in child welfare model acts instead of the negative feature of termination. That was the background for the Model Act to Free Children for Permanent Placement.

Current state termination of parental rights acts generally provide that the state in which the child resides has jurisdiction to entertain a petition for termination. As stated earlier, the standard of proof is at least clear and convincing evidence. Who has standing to petition for termination varies. In addition to state authorities, others may include relatives of the child, the birth parent out of custody, the child's attorney, foster parents, guardian of the child, guardian *ad litem*, and in the unusual case and under statutory authority, the child herself. Whether indigent parents must be appointed legal counsel is a matter of state statute. In *Lassiter v. Department of Social Services*, 452 U.S. 18 (1981), the United States Supreme Court held that indigent parents do not have a constitutional right to appointed counsel. However, a majority of jurisdictions, recognizing the severity and irrevocable nature of the proceeding, do provide for such appointment by statute.

Where a child has remained in the care of the same foster parents for years, a bond often attaches between the child and the foster parents, who then wish to adopt their foster child. Even though the United States Supreme Court in *Smith v. Organization of Foster Families for Equality & Reform*, 431 U.S. 816 (1977) recognized that special relationship, it would not accord foster parents a "liberty interest" in their foster children like birth parents have. Thus the state's denying foster parents notice when their foster child is being returned to her birth parents was not a violation of due process of law. Individual state law might, however, provide such notification if the foster child is in some way related to the foster parent.

During the 1960s and 1970s, foster parents experienced a barrier to their adopting their foster children. The child's availability for adoption was the first problem and that was met by reforming termination of parental rights statutes. What was remaining, however, was the financial problem. Foster care payments were terminated when a foster child was adopted. The financial problem had to be met as well.

B. Subsidized Adoption

The Model Subsidized Adoption Act was designed to provide a financial subsidy to children who were declared "hard to place" for adoption because of their age, their being a part of a sibling group that should be placed together to support the continuity of family relationships, their race or ethnicity or because of special health needs requiring medical attention whether immediate or long-term. The Model Act envisioned a system similar to Social Security in that the recipient of the subsidy would be the child herself. A child would become eligible for a subsidy and certified as such by an appropriate agency if she fell into any of the above categories. Unlike Social Security however, the subsidy would not be a set amount for all children, but would cover financial costs relating to the specific needs of the child who was in the care of the Department of Social Services. For example, if the child was in need of psychiatric services, the subsidy would cover those services as long as they were necessary. If the child needed medical services because of a chronic

medical condition, those services would be covered.
Further, if the child needed remedial educational
services, those would be covered. Under the Model
Act, an adoption subsidy would not be considered a
substitute for monthly foster care payments. Once
again, the aim of subsidized adoption was to facilitate the adoption of a hard to place child under the
care of the state's Department of Social Services
and ordinarily placed with foster parents who, without the subsidy, would not be able to adopt the
child.

All American jurisdictions now have legislation
authorizing subsidized adoptions and those statutes
have similarities with the Model Act. The subsidy
goes to the foster parents who use the funds for
their adopted child's benefit. Subsidy coverage varies according to individual states and the amount
usually may not exceed the monthly foster care
payment and can be revised according to the needs
of the adoptive parents and those of the child. The
Federal Adoption Assistance and Child Welfare Act
of 1980 (Pub. L. No. 96–272.94 Stat. 500, 42 USC
§ 620 *et seq.* (1980)) provides funding to individual
states for subsidies to hard to place children in the
care of a state child welfare agency who enters into
an agreement with the foster parents about the
conditions of the subsidy. The Act sets out requirements for eligibility, the important ones being that
the child could not be placed for adoption without a
subsidy because of the special needs of the child
who also qualifies for assistance under Aid to Families with Dependent Children or Supplemental Se-

curity Income (42 U.S.C. § 673(a)) and the foster parents with whom the child lives are the appropriate adoptive parents. It must be emphasized that the eligibility criteria refer to the characteristics of the child, not those of the prospective adoptive parents, whose income is not relevant.

The Federal Adoption Assistance and Child Welfare Act of 1980 works in concert with state laws. State subsidized adoption laws sometimes cover children that the federal law would not, and state laws sometimes provide benefits unavailable under the federal law. The subsidy ends when the child turns eighteen. However, it can be continued to age twenty-one if the child evidences a mental or physical handicap, and in some cases, beyond that age under the federal Medicaid program.

1.   State Subsidized Adoption Statutes

State	Statute(s)
Alabama	ALA. CODE §§ 26–10–20 to 26–10–30 (2012)
Alaska	ALASKA STAT. §§ 25–23–190 to 25–23–210 (2012)
Arizona	ARIZ. REV. STAT. ANN. §§ 8–141 to 8–161 (2012)
Arkansas	ARK. CODE ANN. §§ 9–9–401 to 9–9–412 (2011)
California	CAL. WELF. & INST. CODE §§ 16115–16123 (2012)
Colorado	COLO. REV. STAT. §§ 26–7–101 to 26–7–108 (2012)
Connecticut	CONN. GEN. STAT. §§ 17A–116 to 17A–121A (2012)

State	Statute(s)
Delaware	DEL. CODE ANN. tit. 31, §§ 304–305 (2011)
District of Columbia*	D.C. CODE ANN. §§ 3–114(a)(3), 3–115 (2012)
Florida	FLA. STAT. § 409.166 (2012)
Georgia	GA. CODE ANN. § 49–5–8(a)(7)(F) (2011)
Hawaii	HAW. REV. STAT. §§ 346–1, 346–301 to 346–305 (2011)
Idaho	IDAHO CODE §§ 56–801 to 56–806 (2012)
Illinois	ILL. COMP. STAT. ANN. tit. 20 § 505/5(j) (2011)
Indiana*	IND. CODE §§ 31–19–26–1 to 31–19–26–6 (2011)
Iowa	IOWA CODE §§ 600.17–600.23 (2012)
Kansas	KAN. STAT. ANN. §§ 38–319 to 38–340 (2012)
Kentucky*	KY. REV. STAT. §§ 199.55, 199.57 (2011)
Louisiana	LA. REV. STAT. §§ 46:1790 to 46:1794 (2011)
Maine	ME. REV. STAT. tit. 18–A §§ 9–402 to 9–404 (2011)
Maryland	MD. FAM. LAW CODE §§ 5–401 to 5–415 (2011)
Massachusetts	MASS. GEN. LAWS ANN. ch. 18B §§ 21, 22 (2012)
Michigan	MICH. COMP. LAWS §§ 400–115f to 400–115m (2012)
Minnesota	MINN. STAT. § 259.67 (2012)
Mississippi	MISS. CODE §§ 93–17–51 to 69 (2011)
Missouri	MO. REV. STAT. §§ 453.065, 453.073, 453.074 (2011)

State	Statute(s)
Montana*	MONT. CODE §§ 52–2–501 to 52–2–528 (2011)
Nebraska	NEB. REV. STAT. §§ 43–117 to 43.118 (2011)
Nevada	NEV. REV. STAT. § 127.186 (2011)
New Hampshire	N.H. REV. STAT. § 170–F:1to F:10 (2011)
New Jersey	N.J. STAT. §§ 30:4C–45 to 30:4C–49 (2012)
New Mexico	N.M. STAT. §§ 32A–5–43 to 32A–5–45 (2011)
New York	N.Y. SOC. SERV. LAWS §§ 450–458 (2011)
North Carolina	N.C. GEN. STAT. §§ 108A–49 to 108A–50 (2011)
North Dakota	N.D. CENT. CODE § 50–09–02.2 (2011)
Ohio	OHIO REV. CODE §§ 5153.16(B)(15), 5153.163 (2011)
Oklahoma	OKLA. STAT. tit. 10 §§ 7510–1.1 to 1.6 (2012)
Oregon	OR. REV. STAT. §§ 418.330, 335, 340 (2012)
Pennsylvania	62 PA. CONS. STAT. §§ 771–774 (2011)
Rhode Island	R.I. GEN. LAWS § 15–7–25 (2011)
South Carolina	S.C. CODE §§ 20–7–1900 to 20–7–1970 (2012)
South Dakota	S.D. CODIFIED LAWS § 28–1–64 (2012)
Tennessee	TENN. CODE ANN. § 37–5–106(13) (2012)
Texas	TEX. FAM. CODE §§ 162–301 to 162–304 (2011)

State	Statute(s)
Utah*	UTAH CODE § 62A–4a–108 (2011)
Vermont	VT. STAT. ANN. tit. 33 § 4903(6) (2012)
Virginia*	VA. CODE ANN. §§ 63.1–238.1 to 238.5 (2012)
Washington	WASH. REV. CODE §§ 74–13–100 to 150 (2012)
West Virginia	W. VA. CODE § 49–2–17 (2012)
Wisconsin	WIS. STAT. § 48–975 (2011)
Wyoming	WYO. STAT. ANN. § 1–22–115 (2011)

* The following statutes have been renumbered as:

- DC: D.C. CODE § 4–301 (2012)
- Indiana: IND. CODE §§ 31–19–26.5–1 to 13 (2011)
- Kentucky: KY. REV. STAT. ANN. §§ 199.555—557 (2011)
- Montana: MONT. CODE §§ 42–10–101 to 42–10–128 (2011)
- Utah: UTAH CODE ANN. § 62A–4a–907 (2011)
- Virginia: VA. CODE ANN. §§ 63.2–1300—1304 (2012)

C. New Assisted Reproductive Technology and Adoption

For years artificial insemination was the alternative to sexual intercourse between a man and a woman for procreation. With this method, the mother is known but the sperm donor may or may not be known depending on the circumstance. Whether a sperm donor has parental rights and obligations is initially a matter to be agreed upon by the parties. However, a court may decide not to honor such an agreement if the result does not further the best interests of the child. Adoption by the sperm donor would be unnecessary since he would be the birth father.

New reproductive techniques have developed that raise questions about status: is the mother of the newborn the person whose egg has been fertilized or the person who has given birth to the child, even though she has no genetic link to the newborn? What rights attach to the gestational carrier, the woman who has no genetic link to the child she is carrying? What rights attach to sperm donors, including the right of privacy? And what about the rights of the children who are born with the new assisted reproductive techniques? Do they have a right to know the identity of their gestational mother as well as the name of the man who donated his sperm to create them? In addition, what are the proprietary rights of the egg donor and sperm donor to the embryo?

When there is no genetic link to either the woman who has provided an egg to be fertilized or to man who has provided his sperm, adoption of the child who has been conceived through the new assisted reproductive techniques may be the appropriate vehicle for parenthood. Issues regarding regulation of new assisted reproductive technology are being raised by state legislatures, and the legal status of the parties who are directly connected to the new technologies are being resolved by state courts as issues arise. In most instances there is no legal model to turn to for guidance as evidenced by the first known surrogacy case to be decided by a state supreme court. The whole area of assisted reproductive technology presents the issue of law responding to science.

1. Embryo Adoption

"Embryo adoption" is the phrase used to describe the practice of donating cryogenically preserved embryos to a genetically unrelated woman for implantation and eventual birth. Referring to the practice as adoption may be a misnomer because the adoption laws do not, in fact, govern it. Since all state adoption laws only allow the placement of a child for adoption after a child has been born, that is not the case in embryo adoption. The law concerning this practice is undeveloped. Alabama, Florida, Georgia, Louisiana, New Hampshire, Ohio and Oklahoma expressly permit embryo adoptions. [ALA. CODE §§ 26–17–702, 704 (West 2012); FLA. STAT. ANN. §§ 742.11(2), 742.14 (West 2012); GA. CODE ANN. §§ 19–8–40 to 43 (West 2011); LA. REV. STAT. ANN. § 9:130 (West. 2011); N.H. REV. STAT. ANN. § 168–B:13 (West 2012); OHIO REV. CODE ANN. § 3111.97 (West 2012); OKLA. STAT. ANN. tit. 10 § 556 (West 2012). These state statutes are designed to regulate the practice, which may raise serious questions of who may avail themselves of this procedure, and who is the legal parent.

a.   Embryo Adoption Statutes

State	Citation	Valid?	Comments
Alabama	ALA. CODE §§ 26–17–701 to 707 (West 2012).	Valid	Alabama law provides that a married couple who, under the supervision of a licensed physician, engage in assisted reproduction through use of donated eggs, sperm, or both, will be treated at law as if they are the sole natural and legal parents of a child conceived thereby. § 26–17–702. Although the law places no other restrictions on embryo adoptions, the law implies that the receiving couple must be married. The husband and wife must each consent to the procedure, and the husband may withdraw consent at any time before placement of the embryo. *See* § 16–17–704.
Alaska	N/A	N/A	N/A
Arizona	N/A	N/A	N/A
Arkansas	N/A	N/A	N/A
California	CAL. HEALTH & SAFETY CODE § 125315 (West 2012).	Presumably Valid	Although California law does not provide express regulations of embryo adoptions, it does contemplate donation of embryos. Under California law, an individual who has undergone fertility treatments and is seeking to dispose of remaining embryos may elect to donate them to another couple or individual. It is

State	Citation	Valid?	Comments
			a criminal offense to implant embryos without the donor's consent.
Colorado	COLO. REV. STAT. ANN. § 19–4–106 (West 2012).	Presumably Valid	Although Colorado law does not expressly govern embryo adoptions, it insulates sperm or egg donors from parental rights and liabilities. It is possible that Colorado law covers embryo donors as well, but there is no case law on this point.
Connecticut	CONN. GEN. STAT. ANN. § 19a–32d (West 2012).	Presumably Valid	Although Connecticut law does not provide express regulations on embryo adoptions, it does contemplate donation of embryos. Under Connecticut law, an individual who has undergone fertility treatments and is seeking to dispose of remaining embryos may elect to donate them to another person. The statute criminalizes the sale of embryos for research purposes, as well as the sale of unfertilized eggs and/or sperm. It does not, however, explicitly criminalize the sale of embryos for the purpose of assisted reproduction.
Delaware	DEL. CODE ANN. tit. 13, §§ 8–101 to 904 (West 2011).	Presumably Valid	Although Delaware law does not expressly govern embryo adoptions, it has adopted the Uniform

State	Citation	Valid?	Comments
			Parentage Act, which insulates a "donor" from parental responsibility of a child born by means of assisted reproduction. § 8–702. "Assisted reproduction" is defined to include embryo donation. § 8–102. Because Delaware law provides that a mother-child relationship is established by the mother's having given birth to a child, and that a father-child relationship is established by the father's having consented to assisted reproduction, it is likely that Delaware law permits embryo adoption by a consenting couple. *See* § 8–201.
District of Columbia	N/A	N/A	N/A
Florida	FLA. STAT. ANN. § 742.11(2) (West 2012).	Valid	In Florida, a child born to a married couple who has been conceived by means of preembryos is irrebuttably presumed to be the child of the recipient gestating woman and her husband, provided that both parties have consented in writing to the use of preembryos. Florida permits "reasonable compensation" directly related to the donation of preembryos.
Georgia	GA. CODE ANN. §§ 19–8–40 to 43 (West 2011).	Valid	Georgia provides regulations for embryo adoptions and allows

State	Citation	Valid?	Comments
			for embryos to have the legal right to an adoption as a human being. Georgia impliedly elevates the status of embryos to legal persons.
Hawaii	N/A	N/A	N/A
Idaho	N/A	N/A	N/A
Illinois	N/A	N/A	N/A
Indiana	IND. CODE ANN. § 35–46–5–3 (West 2011).	Presumably Valid	Although Indiana law does not expressly permit embryo adoption, it does make it a felony to purchase or sell a human embryo.
Iowa	N/A	N/A	N/A
Kansas	N/A	N/A	N/A
Kentucky	N/A	N/A	N/A
Louisiana	LA. REV. STAT. ANN. § 9:130 (West 2011).	Valid	Louisiana permits in vitro fertilized human ova to be available for adoptive implantation in accordance with written procedures of the facility where they are housed or stored. An embryo is considered a "juridical person which cannot be owned by the in vitro fertilization patients who owe it a high duty of care and prudent administration." No compensation may be paid.
Maine	N/A	N/A	N/A
Maryland	N/A	N/A	N/A
Massachusetts	MASS. GEN. LAWS ANN. ch. 111L, §§ 4, 8 (West 2012).	Presumably Valid	Although Massachusetts law does not provide express regulations on embryo adoptions, it does contemplate donation of embryos. Under Massachusetts law,

State	Citation	Valid?	Comments
			an individual who has undergone fertility treatments and is seeking to dispose of remaining embryos may elect to donate them to another person.
			It is unlawful to purchase or sell embryos for research purposes, but the law does not expressly prohibit the sale of embryos for adoption.
Michigan	N/A	N/A	N/A
Minnesota	N/A	N/A	N/A
Mississippi	N/A	N/A	N/A
Missouri	N/A	N/A	N/A
Montana	N/A	N/A	N/A
Nebraska	N/A	N/A	N/A
Nevada	N/A	N/A	N/A
New Hampshire	N.H. REV. STAT. ANN. § 168–B:13 (West 2011).	Valid	New Hampshire law provides that women 21 years of age or older may receive a preembryo transfer, but New Hampshire law does not provide any further regulations on embryo adoptions.
New Jersey	N.J. STAT. ANN. § 26:2Z–2 (West 2012).	Presumably Valid	New Jersey law permits individuals to donate embryos to other individuals following infertility treatment. New Jersey, however, provides no other regulations on embryo adoptions.
New Mexico	N/A	N/A	N/A
New York	N/A	N/A	N/A
North Carolina	N/A	N/A	N/A
North Dakota	N.D. CENT. CODE §§ 14–20–01 to	Presumably Valid	Although North Dakota law does not ex-

State	Citation	Valid?	Comments
	14–20–66 (West 2011).		pressly govern embryo adoptions, it has adopted the Uniform Parentage Act, which insulates a "donor" from parental responsibility of a child born by means of assisted reproduction. § 14–20–60. "Assisted reproduction" is defined to include embryo donation. § 14–20–02. Because North Dakota law provides that a mother-child relationship is established by the mother's having given birth to a child, and that a father-child relationship is established by the father's having consented to assisted reproduction, it is likely that North Dakota law permits embryo adoption by a consenting couple. *See* § 14–20–07.
Ohio	Ohio Rev. Code Ann. § 3111.97 (West 2011).	Valid	Ohio law provides that a "woman who gives birth to a child born as a result of embryo donation shall be treated in law and regarded as the natural mother of the child." The law also provides that a consenting husband "shall be treated in law and regarded as the natural father of the child." Ohio does not, however, provide any other regulations on embryo adoption.
Oklahoma	Okla. Stat. Ann. tit. 10, § 556	Valid	Embryo adoption, or "embryo transfer,"

State	Citation	Valid?	Comments
	(West 2012).		is permissible in Oklahoma. Written consent is required by all parties involved—both the couple receiving the embryo as well as the couple donating it. The consent of the couple desiring to receive the embryo must be executed and acknowledged by the donating couple, the physician performing the technique, and a judge. Upon birth, the donating couple is relieved of all parenting responsibilities. Moreover, the embryo must be donated; compensation is prohibited.
Oregon	N/A	N/A	N/A
Pennsylvania	N/A	N/A	N/A
Rhode Island	N/A	N/A	N/A
South Carolina	N/A	N/A	N/A
South Dakota	N/A	N/A	N/A
Tennessee	N/A	N/A	N/A
Texas	TEX. FAM. CODE ANN. §§ 160.102, 160.702, 160.763 (Vernon 2011).	Presumably valid	Although no Texas law specifically governs embryo adoption, its version of the Uniform Parentage Act defines "assisted reproduction" to include "donation of embryos." § 160.102. The statute also provides that donors are not the parents of a child conceived by means of assisted reproduction. § 160.702. Also, the statute requires

State	Citation	Valid?	Comments
			that health care facilities report the number of embryos created for assisted reproduction that were not transferred. § 160.763. Thus, embryo adoptions are impliedly permissible under Texas law.
Utah	UTAH CODE ANN. §§ 78B–15–102,-702, 703 (West 2011).	Presumably Valid	Although Utah law does not expressly govern embryo adoptions, it has adopted the Uniform Parentage Act, which insulates a donor from parental responsibility of a child born by means of assisted reproduction. § 78B–15–702. The statute defines "assisted reproduction" to include embryo donation. § 78B–15–102. Because Utah law provides that a mother-child relationship is established by the mother's having given birth to a child, and that a father-child relationship is established by the father's having consented to assisted reproduction, it is likely that Utah law permits embryo adoption by a consenting couple. *See* § 78B–15–703.
Vermont	N/A	N/A	N/A
Virginia	VA. CODE ANN. §§ 20–156 to 158 (West 2012).	Presumably Valid	Although Virginia law does not expressly govern embryo adoptions, it includes embryo transfers within the definition of "assisted concep-

State	Citation	Valid?	Comments
			tion." § 20–156. The law provides that the gestational mother and her husband are the parents of a child born by means of assisted conception, and that a donor does not have parental responsibility for the child. § 20–158. Thus, embryo adoptions likely are valid in Virginia.
Washington	WASH. REV. CODE ANN. §§ 26.26.011—.913 (West 2012).	Presumably Valid	Although Washington law does not expressly govern embryo adoptions, it has adopted the Uniform Parentage Act, which insulates a donor from parental responsibility of a child born by means of assisted reproduction. § 26.26.705. The statute defines "assisted reproduction" to include embryo donation. § 26.26.011. Because Washington law provides that a mother-child relationship is established by the mother's having given birth to a child, and that a father-child relationship is established by the father's having consented to assisted reproduction, it is likely that Washington law permits embryo adoption by a consenting couple. *See* § 26.26.101.
			The Washington Supreme Court has upheld an individual's right to place pre-em-

State	Citation	Valid?	Comments
			bryos up for adoption. *See Litowitz v. Litowitz*, 48 P.3d 261 (Wash. 2002).
West Virginia	N/A	N/A	N/A
Wisconsin	N/A	N/A	N/A
Wyoming	WYO. STAT. ANN. §§ 14–2–401 to 907 (West 2011).	Presumably Valid	Although Wyoming law does not expressly govern embryo adoptions, it does insulate a donor from parental responsibility of a child born by means of assisted reproduction. § 14–2–902. The statute defines "assisted reproduction" to include embryo donation. § 14–2–402. Because Wyoming law provides that a mother-child relationship is established by the mother's having given birth to a child, and that a father-child relationship is established by the father's having consented to assisted reproduction, it is likely that Wyoming law permits embryo adoption by a consenting couple. *See* § 14–2–501.

2. Surrogacy

When *In re Baby M,* 537 A.2d 1227 (N.J. 1988) was decided by the Supreme Court of New Jersey, the facts of the case must have presented a dilemma to the litigants and to the court in terms of their fitting into a conventional legal model for purposes of providing a remedy. In the case, a married woman, Mrs. Whitehead, and a married man, Mr. Stern, who were not married to each other, entered into a contract which included an exchange of promises in which Mrs. Whitehead agreed to be artificially inseminated with Mr. Stern's semen, conceiving a child, carrying the child to term and after the birth of the child, surrendering the child to Mr. Stern and his wife. Additionally, Mrs. Whitehead agreed to fulfill the legal requirements for the termination of her rights so that Mrs. Stern could adopt the child. After the baby girl was born, Mrs. Whitehead was listed as the mother of the child on the birth records, and contrary to fact, Mr. Whitehead was listed as the birth father. Mrs. Whitehead did, in fact, surrender her baby girl to the Sterns, but also asked that she be allowed to have the child for a week. Not realizing that Mrs. Whitehead had changed her mind about relinquishing her daughter, the Sterns agreed only to regret their decision when Mrs. Whitehead refused to return her daughter. A dispute resulted and Mr. Stern sought legal action to enforce the agreement, mandate that Mrs. Whitehead's custodial rights be terminated according to the terms of the agreement, and allow Mrs. Stern to adopt the child.

The New Jersey trial court held that the surrogacy contract was valid and ordered the termination of Mrs. Whitehead's parental rights, granted custody to Mr. Stern and, after a hearing, allowed the child's adoption by Mrs. Stern. That decision was appealed and the New Jersey Supreme Court reversed the decision, holding that the surrogacy agreement was invalid, and remanded the case to the Superior Court to determine which of the two legal parents—Mrs. Whitehead or Mr. Stern—should be granted custody. That court decided that custody of the child should be awarded to Mr. Stern with visitation rights to Mrs. Whitehead. At that stage, the result resembled a divorce outcome with the birth parents, not married to each other and no doubt antagonistic toward each other, having a continuing relationship through the child. Mrs. Stern became the functional equivalent of a step-parent. Ultimately, the child became fully integrated into the Stern family, although she had two mothers.

Mrs. Whitehead assumed the role of a "gestational surrogate," which involved her ova being fertilized by the sperm of a man to whom she was not married but who desired to be the father of the child and whose wife desired to be the child's mother. In the situation where the surrogate has no genetic connection to the child she is carrying, a serious questions is raised as to who is the legal mother. Typically, the woman who gives birth to the child is considered the mother and her name appears on the birth certificate of the newborn. That rule was developed before the assisted reproduction techniques existed. In *Johnson v. Calvert,* 851 P.2d 776 (Cal. 1993), a woman, unrelated to either Mr. or Mrs. Calvert agreed to have an embryo created by the couples' sperm and egg implanted in her uterus so that she could gestate a child for the couple. The arrangement was memorialized in a contract in which the Calverts promised to pay the surrogate mother a certain amount of money in installments lasting after the birth of the child who was to be surrendered to the Calverts. Relations between the three parties became strained when accusations were made by the Calverts about Anna Johnson's not disclosing certain personal facts about her health and ability to carry a fetus to term and by Anna Johnson about the Calverts not obtaining the required insurance policy. Ultimately, the surrogate mother made threats and refused to surrender the child unless the balance of the payments due her were paid. The Calverts responded by bringing a law suit seeking a declaration that they were the legal parents of the unborn child. Anna Johnson sought a declaration that she was the child's mother. Two months later the child was born and the following month a trial judge decided that the Calverts were "the child's genetic, biological and natural father and mother" and Anna Johnson had no parental rights. A California Appeals Court affirmed the trial courts' decision and the California Supreme Court agreed. In affirming the Appeals Court's decision, the court rejected the argument that surrogacy contracts violated the state's social policy and other traditional arguments against surrogacy, like dehumanizing women, promoting fraud in the inducement to act as a surrogate or devaluing children and treating them like property. Further, the court went on to say that the California adoption statute did not apply given the fact pattern of surrogacy contract arrangements. Additionally, the court was unwilling to accept the proposition that the child had two mothers. In California, the gestational carrier, genetically unrelated to the newborn infant, is not the mother of the child. The *Calvert* case has implications for fact patterns that include gestational carriers who are unrelated to the newborn infant child who was conceived by using the egg of another woman and the sperm of a man in a same-sex marital relationship. Adoption would seem appropriate where the intended parents are not biologically related to the infant.

In the situation in which a male same-sex married couple enters into an agreement with a surrogate to carry to term a fetus not genetically related to either man, both would have to adopt the child if the jurisdiction in which the adoption were to occur recognized the rights of same-sex married couples. In situations in which a woman in a same-sex marriage has carried to term a fetus of whom she is the genetic mother, her spouse would have to adopt the child. The *Calvert* case has implications for fact patterns that include gestational carriers who are unrelated to the newborn infant child who was conceived by using the egg of another woman and the sperm of a man in a same-sex marital relationship. Adoption would seem appropriate where the intended parents are not related to the infant.

Surrogacy is a controversial method for achieving parenthood for many of the reasons stated in the *Calvert* case. For example, it has been said that surrogacy arrangements dehumanize woman by treating them as merely vessels for the production of children. They commercialize the process of reproduction by masking the fact that there has been a transfer of money not only for the medical costs for the procedure but for the actual job of carrying a fetus to term. There is a belief that the new reproductive technologies have advanced beyond where society is in terms of morality and the kind of society people desire. For all those reasons, laws regulating surrogacy agreements are not uniform.

a. State Surrogacy Statutes

State	Citations	Valid?	Comments
Alabama	ALA. CODE §§ 26–10A–34(a)–(c) (West 2012).	Presumably valid	The Alabama Adoption Code criminalizes the payment of money for the placement for adoption, for the consent to an adoption, and for cooperation in the completion of an adoption of a child. It specifically exempts, however, surrogacy motherhood.
Alaska	N/A	N/A	N/A
Arizona	ARIZ. REV. STAT. ANN. § 25–218 (West 2012).	Invalid	Arizona law provides that "[n]o person may enter into, induce, arrange, procure, or otherwise assist in the formation of a surrogate parentage contract." Further, it provides that "[a] surrogate is the legal mother of a child born as a result of a surrogate parentage contract and is entitled to custody of that child."

State	Citations	Valid?	Comments
			Despite an intermediate appellate court's finding that the statute is unconstitutional on other grounds, the statute continues to exist. *See Soos v. Superior Ct. of Ariz.*, 897 P.2d 1356, 1359 (Ariz. Ct. App. 1994).
Arkansas	ARK. CODE ANN. § 9–10–201 (West 2011).	Presumably valid	The Arkansas Code does not address surrogacy contracts, but creates a presumption that a child born to a surrogate mother is the child of the intended mother and the biological father.
California	*Johnson v. Calvert*, 851 P.2d 776 (Cal. 1993).	Valid	In the gestational surrogacy context, the court looks to the intent of the parties to determine parentage. *See Johnson v. Calvert*, 851 P.2d 776 (Cal. 1993). In traditional surrogacy cases where the surrogate mother is both the biological and birth mother, however, at least one intermediate appellate court has declined to enforce a surrogacy contract because the surrogate did not formally consent to an adoption in the presence of a social worker. *See Moschetta v. Moschetta*, 30 Cal. Rptr.2d 893 (App. 1994).
Colorado	N/A	N/A	N/A
Connecticut	CONN. GEN. STAT. ANN. § 7–48a (West 2012).	Presumably valid	The statute provides that "birth certificate[s] shall be filed with the name of the

State	Citations	Valid?	Comments
			birth mother recorded. If the birth is subject to a gestational agreement, the Department of Public Health shall create a replacement certificate in accordance with an order from a court of competent jurisdiction not later than forty-five days after receipt of such order or forty-five days after the birth of the child, whichever is later." At least one court, however, has held that section 7–48a does not guarantee an "unqualified enforcement of private gestational agreements." *See Oleski v. Hynes*, 2008 WL 2930518, at 11 (Conn. Super. Ct. 2008).
Delaware	N/A	N/A	N/A
District of Columbia	D.C. CODE §§ 16–401,402 (West 2012).	Invalid	The D.C. Code prohibits surrogate parent contracts. The statute provides that "surrogate parenting contracts are prohibited and rendered unenforceable in the District." Moreover, any person who "is involved in, or induces, arranges, or otherwise assists in the formation of a surrogate parenting contract for a fee, compensation, or other remuneration . . . shall be subject to a civil penalty not to exceed $10,000 or imprisonment for not more than 1 year, or

State	Citations	Valid?	Comments
			both." "Surrogate parenting contract" means any agreement in which a "woman agrees either to be artificially inseminated with the sperm of a man who is not her husband, or to be impregnated with an embryo that is the product of an ovum fertilization with the sperm of a man who is not her husband."
Florida	FLA. STAT. ANN. § 742.15 (West 2012).	Valid (gestational surrogacy only)	Gestational contracts are valid only if intended mother "cannot physically gestate a pregnancy to term" or "the gestation will cause a risk to the physical health of the intended mother" or fetus. The intended parents "may agree to pay only reasonable living, legal, medical, psychological, and psychiatric expenses of the gestational surrogate that are directly related to prenatal, intrapartal, and postpartal periods."
			Impliedly, the Florida statute prohibits gestational egg and sperm donor surrogacy by requiring that at least one of the intended parents be genetically related to the child.
Georgia	N/A	N/A	N/A
Hawaii	N/A	N/A	N/A
Idaho	N/A	N/A	N/A

State	Citations	Valid?	Comments
Illinois	750 ILL. COMP. STAT. ANN. 47/1–75 (West 2011) [Gestational Surrogacy Act].	Valid (gestational surrogacy only)	The Illinois statute protects only gestational surrogacy contracts where the surrogate mother has no biological relation to the child. At least one of the intended parents must be biologically related to the child. The surrogate mother must be at least 21 years old, have undergone legal/psychological consultation, and have given birth at least once before. The Act does not place explicit limitations on compensation.
Indiana	IND. CODE ANN. §§ 31–20–1–1, 31–20–1–2 (West 2011).	Invalid	Indiana law provides that "it is against public policy to enforce any term of a surrogate agreement that requires a surrogate to . . . become pregnant."
Iowa	IOWA CODE ANN. § 710.11 (West 2012).	Presumably Valid	The Iowa Code makes it a felony to sell or attempt to sell an individual, but creates an exception for surrogate mother arrangements. "Surrogate mother arrangements" means "an arrangement whereby a female agrees to be artificially inseminated with the semen of a donor, to bear a child, and to relinquish all rights regarding that child to the donor or donor couple." Thus, traditional surrogacy agreements are presumptively valid in Iowa, but the law

State	Citations	Valid?	Comments
			does not provide whether gestational surrogacy agreements also are exempted.
Kansas	N/A	N/A	N/A
Kentucky	KY. REV. STAT. ANN. § 199.590(4) (West 2011).	Presumably Valid	The Kentucky statute expressly prohibits compensated traditional surrogacy contracts. The law provides that "[a] person, agency, institution, or intermediary shall not be a party to a contract or agreement which would compensate a woman for her artificial insemination and subsequent termination of parental rights to a child born as a result of that artificial insemination." Uncompensated surrogacy agreements, however, presumably are enforceable.
Louisiana	LA. REV. STAT. ANN. § 9:2713 (West 2011).	Valid	Louisiana law prohibits compensated surrogacy agreements. The law provides that "any agreement whereby a person not married to the contributor of the sperm agrees for valuable consideration to be inseminated, to carry any resulting fetus to birth, and then to relinquish to the contributor of the sperm the custody and all rights and obligations to the child" shall be null and void. Uncompensated surrogacy contracts, how-

State	Citations	Valid?	Comments
			ever, generally are enforceable.
Maine	N/A	N/A	N/A
Maryland	MD. CODE ANN., CRIM. LAW § 3–603 (West 2012); MD. CODE ANN., FAM. LAW § 5–3B–32 (West 2012).	Presumably Valid	There are no Maryland statutes that expressly protect surrogacy agreements. Compensated surrogacy agreements, however, are unlawful and may be criminally prosecuted. *See In re Roberto d.B.*, 923 A.2d 115 (Md. 2007). This prohibition does not include compensation for medical or legal services. At common law, gestational surrogacy agreements are enforceable. It is unclear whether traditional surrogacy agreements are enforceable as well.
Massachusetts	*R.R. v. M.H.*, 689 N.E.2d 790 (Mass. 1998); *Culliton v. Beth Israel Deaconess Med. Ctr.*, 756 N.E.2d 1133 (Mass. 2001).	Valid	There are no statutes in Massachusetts governing surrogacy In *R.R.*, the Supreme Judicial Court noted that traditional surrogacy agreements are enforceable and are governed by the Massachusetts adoption statute. *See* MASS. GEN. LAWS ANN. ch. 210, § 2 (West 2009). Applying the adoption statute, a surrogate mother must consent to the adoption of her child no sooner than four days *after* birth. The court noted that a surrogate mother should not be compensated beyond

State	Citations	Valid?	Comments
			pregnancy-related expenses.
			In *Culliton*, the SJC held that the adoption statute does not govern gestational surrogacy agreements, and authorized the Family and Probate Court to enter pre-birth judgments declaring the child's mother and father in the gestational surrogacy context.
Michigan	MICH. COMP. LAWS ANN. §§ 722.855–.859 (West 2012).	Invalid	Michigan law provides that "[a] surrogate parentage contract is void and unenforceable as contrary to public policy." Moreover, parties that enter into compensated surrogacy agreements may be prosecuted criminally. The law provides that a participating party "who knowingly enters into a surrogate parentage contract for compensation is guilty of a misdemeanor punishable by a fine of not more than $10,000.00 or imprisonment for not more than 1 year, or both." A person other than a participating party "who induces, arranges, procures, or otherwise assists in the formation of a surrogate parentage contract for compensation is guilty of a

State	Citations	Valid?	Comments
			felony punishable by a fine of not more than $50,000.00 or imprisonment for not more than 5 years, or both."
Minnesota	N/A	N/A	N/A
Mississippi	N/A	N/A	N/A
Missouri	N/A	N/A	N/A
Montana	N/A	N/A	N/A
Nebraska	NEB. REV. STAT. § 25–21.200 (West 2011).	Presumably Valid	The Nebraska statute expressly prohibits the enforcement of surrogacy parenthood contracts, but defines a "surrogate parenthood contract" to mean "a contract by which a woman is to be compensated for bearing a child of a man who is not her husband." Presumably, *unpaid* surrogacy agreements are valid in Nebraska.
Nevada	NEV. REV. STAT. ANN. § 126.045 (West 2011).	Valid	The Nevada statute expressly permits surrogacy agreements. It is unlawful to pay or offer to pay money or anything of value to the surrogate except for pregnancy-related medical and necessary expenses. Because the statute defines "assisted conception" as a pregnancy resulting when an egg and sperm from the intended parents are placed in a surrogate through the intervention of medical technology, it is possible that the statute applies only

State	Citations	Valid?	Comments
			to gestational surrogacy agreements.
New Hampshire	N.H. REV. STAT. ANN. §§ 168–B:1 to B:32 (West 2011).	Valid	New Hampshire law expressly permits surrogacy agreements. The agreements, however, must be judicially preauthorized. Fees are limited to pregnancy-related expenses, lost wages, health insurance during pregnancy term, and reasonable attorney's and counseling fees. The surrogate mother may exercise her right to keep child up to 72 hours after birth. The statute impliedly prohibits gestational surrogacy by gamete donation (where neither the surrogate nor the intended parents are genetically or biologically related to the child).
New Jersey	*In re Baby M.*, 537 A.2d 1227 (N.J. 1988).	Valid	There are no statutes regulating surrogacy adoptions in New Jersey. Surrogacy agreements, however, generally are permitted at common law. In New Jersey, traditional surrogacy agreements are enforceable under adoption laws if the surrogate is not compensated. In addition, binding agreements to surrender the child upon birth are unenforceable. Rather, the surrogate mother must wait 72

State	Citations	Valid?	Comments
			hours after birth to surrender the child.
			At least one trial court has imposed the above restrictions to gestational surrogacy agreements as well. *See A.H.W. v. G.H.B.*, 772 A.2d 948 (N.J. Super. Ct. Ch. Div. 2000).
New Mexico	N/A	N/A	N/A
New York	N.Y. DOM. REL. LAW § 122 (McKinney 2011).	Invalid	By statute, surrogacy parenting contracts are void and unenforceable in New York. The law provides that "[s]urrogate parenting contracts are hereby declared contrary to the public policy of this state, and are void and unenforceable." The statute defines "surrogate parenting contract" to include compensated and uncompensated surrogacy agreements.
North Carolina	N/A	N/A	N/A
North Dakota	N.D. CENT. CODE § 14–18–05 (West 2011).	Invalid	Under North Dakota law, surrogacy agreements are void and unenforceable. The law provides that "any agreement in which a woman agrees to become a surrogate or to relinquish that woman's rights and duties as parent of a child conceived through assisted conception is void."

State	Citations	Valid?	Comments
			In the event that a surrogacy is arranged, the surrogate is the mother of a resulting child and the surrogate's husband, if a party to the agreement, is the father of the child. If the surrogate's husband is not a party to the agreement or the surrogate is unmarried, paternity of the child is governed by the Uniform Parentage Act.
Ohio	*J.F. v. D.B.*, 879 N.E.2d 740 (Ohio 2007).	Valid	There are no statutes in Ohio regulating surrogacy adoptions. At common law, however, *gestational* surrogacy agreements are valid and enforceable. In *J.F. v. D.B.*, the Ohio Supreme Court held that gestational surrogacy agreements do not violate Ohio public policy, even when a provision of the agreement prohibits the gestational surrogate from asserting parental rights upon birth. Interestingly, the Ohio Supreme Court did not discuss the fact that the parties in the case agreed to pay the surrogate $20,000 plus expenses. *See J.F. v. D.B.*, 848 N.E.2d 873 (Ohio Ct. App. 2006). Thus, compensated gestational surrogacy agreements are presumably valid in Ohio.

State	Citations	Valid?	Comments
			The court noted that it was not extending its holding to traditional surrogacy agreements, where the surrogate, whose pregnancy involves her own egg, may have a stronger legal position than a gestational surrogate.
Oklahoma	OKLA. STAT. ANN. tit. 21, § 866 (West 2012).	Presumably valid	Oklahoma law criminalizes the payment of any compensation in exchange for adoption of a minor child. A formal opinion by the Oklahoma Attorney General interprets the prohibition to forbid only the payment of compensation pursuant to a gestational surrogacy contract. This interpretation, however, allows for the payment of pregnancy-related expenses. There is no available case law interpreting this provision of the Oklahoma Statutes.
Oregon	OR. REV. STAT. ANN. § 109.311 (West 2012).	Presumably valid	Oregon law prohibits the payment of a fee for locating a child for adoption. As interpreted by one appellate court, the law does not prohibit the enforcement of a traditional surrogacy agreement, even if the surrogate is compensated beyond pregnancy-related expenses. *See Matter of Adoption of Baby A.*, 877 P.2d 107 (Or. Ct. App. 1994). The court

State	Citations	Valid?	Comments
			implied that compensation is permissible so long as it does not induce the surrogate to enter into a surrogacy agreement.
			In addition, Oregon law expressly exempts fees paid pursuant to a surrogacy agreement from a criminal provision prohibiting the buying and selling of minor children.
Pennsylvania	N/A	N/A	There are no statutes in Pennsylvania regulating surrogacy agreements. At least one intermediate appellate court, however, has declined to declare a gestational surrogacy contract void in Pennsylvania. *See J.F. v. D.B.*, 897 A.2d 1261 (Pa. Super. Ct. 2006). In *J.F.*, a couple entered into a surrogacy arrangement with a third party in Indiana. The appellate court declined to declare the contract null and void on public policy grounds. It noted, however, that its holding was limited to the facts of that particular case, and declined to rule on the validity of surrogacy contracts generally.
Rhode Island	N/A	N/A	N/A
South Carolina	N/A	N/A	N/A
South Dakota	N/A	N/A	N/A

State	Citations	Valid?	Comments
Tennessee	N/A	N/A	N/A
Texas	TEX. FAM. CODE ANN. §§ 160.751–763 (Vernon 2011).	Valid (gestational surrogacy only)	Gestational surrogacy agreements are valid and enforceable under Texas law. A gestational surrogacy agreement must be validated by a judge in order to be enforceable. Texas law also requires that the intended parents be married and that each intended parent be a party to the agreement. The agreement must be validated 14 days prior to the transfer of eggs to the gestational mother. Finally, the gestational mother may terminate the agreement prior to becoming pregnant. Texas law does not apply to traditional surrogacy agreements.
Utah	UTAH CODE ANN. §§ 78B–15–801 to 809 (West 2011).	Valid (gestational surrogacy only)	Gestational surrogacy agreements are valid and enforceable under Utah law. Utah law requires that gestational surrogacy agreements be validated by a judge and that the intended parents be married. Each intended parent must be a party to the agreement. Finally, the gestational mother may terminate the agreement prior to becoming pregnant. Utah law does not apply to traditional

State	Citations	Valid?	Comments
			surrogacy agreements.
Vermont	N/A	N/A	N/A
Virginia	VA. CODE ANN. §§ 20–156 to 20–165 (West 2012).	Valid	Surrogacy agreements, both traditional and gestational, are valid in Virginia. Virginia, however, prefers that agreements are pre-approved by a court. The intended mother must be infertile, unable to bear a child, or unable to do so without unreasonable risk to the unborn child or to the physical or mental health of the intended mother of the child. In addition, at least one of the intended parents must be the biological parent of the child. The agreement also must contain a provision providing for compensation for pregnancy-related costs, but other provisions for compensation are void and unenforceable. The surrogate may terminate the agreement prior to becoming pregnant.
Washington	WASH. REV. CODE ANN. §§ 26.26.021, 210—260 (West 2012).	Valid	Traditional and gestational surrogacy agreements are valid and enforceable under Washington law. The law prohibits, however, the payment of compensation in a surrogacy arrangement. Inten-

State	Citations	Valid?	Comments
			tional violations of the surrogacy law constitute a gross misdemeanor.
			In addition, custody disputes arising from a surrogacy agreement are resolved by the court under Washington's marriage dissolution law.
West Virginia	W. VA. CODE ANN. § 48–22–803 (West 2012).	Presumably valid	Surrogacy agreements are explicitly exempted from provisions making it a crime to sell babies, but no statute explicitly renders surrogacy agreements valid and enforceable.
Wisconsin	WIS. STAT. ANN. § 69.14 (West 2011).	Presumably valid	Under Wisconsin law, a surrogate mother's name is entered on the birth certificate of the child. The law provides, however, that a court may determine parental rights over the child, order that a new birth certificate be created, and that the old certificate be destroyed. The statute, thus, implies that surrogacy agreements are enforceable
Wyoming	N/A	N/A	N/A

D. Second Parent Adoption

Second parent adoption, which is available in twenty-six jurisdictions, ordinarily refers to the situation in which the partner or spouse of the birth mother in a same-sex relationship adopts the child of her partner or spouse without terminating the parental rights of the birth parent. This may occur when the birth mother has been artificially inseminated, given birth and then the partner or spouse wishes to share parenting and have the legal protection of a legal parent. In a certain sense, second parent adoption is similar to step-parent adoption where one spouse is permitted to adopt the birth or adopted child of the other spouse without terminating the parental rights of that spouse.

Second parent adoption is authorized by statute in California [CAL. FAM. CODE § 9000(d)], Colorado [COLO. REV. STAT. § 19–5 203 (1) (d.5)], Connecticut [CONN. GEN. STAT. ANN. § 45a–724 (a) (3), and Vermont [VT. STAT. ANN. tit. 15A § 1–102]. The seven states that authorize second-parent adoption through judicial opinion are: Illinois [*In re Petition of K.M. & D.M.*, 653 N.E.2d 888 (Ill. App. Ct. 1995)], Indiana [*In re Adoption of K.S.P.*, 804 N.E.2d 1253 (Ind. Ct. App. 2004) and *In re Adoption of M.M.G.C.*, 785 N.E.2d 267 (Ind. Ct. App. 2003)], Massachusetts [*In re Adoption of Tammy*, 619 N.E.2d 315 (Mass. 1993)], New Jersey [*In re the Adoption of Two Children by H.N.R.*, 666 A.2d 535 (N.J. Super. 1995)], New York [*In re Jacob, In re Dana*, 660 N.E.2d 397 (N.Y. 1995)], Pennsylvania [*In re Adoption of R.B.F. & R.C.F.*, 803 A.2d 1195 (Pa. 2002)] and the District of Columbia [*In re M.M.D. v. B.H.M.* 662 A.2d 837 (D.C. 1995)].

The Vermont case of *Adoption of B.L.V.B. & E.L.V.B.*, 628 A.2d 1271 (Vt. 1993), pre-dates that state's statute authorizing second-parent adoptions.

In that case two women who had decided to raise children together decided to use the sperm from an anonymous donor so that one of them could give birth to a baby. Although the couple wanted to co-parent the infant, Vermont's adoption statute did not authorize an unmarried, non-birth parent to adopt. Nevertheless, the Vermont Supreme Court allowed the adoption of the infant by the non-birth woman under the step-parent exception. The under-lying basis for the decisions allowing second-parent adoption is the judicial belief that the result will further the child's best interests.

Those states that prohibit second-parent adoption are Nebraska [*In re. Adoption of Luke*, 640 N.W.2d 374 (Neb. 2002)], Ohio [In re Adoption of Doe, 719 N.E.2d 1071 (Ohio Ct. App. 1998)], and Wisconsin [*Interest of Angel Lace M.* 516 N.W.2d 678 (Wis. 1994)]. The decisions rejecting second-parent adop-tion, except by step-parents, are based on the prin-ciple that to allow an adoption without the birth parent relinquishing her rights requires legislative action. In many states, the status of second-parent adoption is unclear, mainly because the highest court in the state has not ruled on it or the legisla-ture of the state has not considered it.

E.   Standards for Placement

Standards for placement are statutory and in cases of agency placement, they are determined by the agency itself. For example, statutory standards may include husband and wife together, an unmar-ried adult, foster parents, a single adult, relatives or stepparents. They may also include a minimum age for the adoptive parent or parents, usually 18, the age of majority. In some jurisdictions the adoptive parent and the adopted child must have a certain year spread between them, like for example, the adopted parent must be ten years older than the adopted child. A disabled person may qualify as an adoptive or foster parent and cannot be rejected specifically because of a disability. In fact, The Americans With Disabilities Act of 1990. § 202, 402 U.S.C.A. § 12132 states that in order to establish a *prima facie* case, an applicant for adoption who has been rejected must show that: (1) she has a disability; (2) she is a qualified individual; and (3) she was discriminated against because of the disability. In *Adams v. Monroe County Dept. of Social Services*, 21 F. Supp. 2d 235 (W.D.N.Y. 1998), a blind woman and her husband who were found unsuitable to become foster parents sued the county agency. The federal court held that the agency had not discriminated against the couple, because there were legitimate concerns about the woman's blindness, especially since she would have been the principal caretaker. The court stated, ''A vast body of case law from new York state courts shows that in matters involving adoption or foster care, it is the child's best interests that are paramount ... Thus [the agency's] role here was not to find a child for plaintiffs' home, but the opposite: to find suitable homes for children. In doing so, [the agency's] determination that it would not be in the available children's best interests to be placed in plaintiffs' home because of the risk of physical harm did not constitute unlawful discrimination." *Id.* at 240. Florida, Idaho, New York and Wisconsin specifically refer to the eligibility of disabled persons to adopt in their statutes. (See FLA. STAT. ANN. § 63.042(4); IDAHO CODE ANN. § 16–1501(a) and (b); N.Y., DOM. REL. LAW § 110; WIS. STAT. ANN. § 48.82(5).

In jurisdictions that allow a birth mother to place her child with an adoptive couple, the choice of parent rests with the birth mother. Agency placements, however, are different. The standards agencies have chosen to select prospective adoptive parents for an available child have varied for the past half century. During the period of adoption history when the goal of adoption was to provide a child for a childless couple, often to provide an heir, the term "matching" was often used to describe the placement process. The idea was to match a child who physically resembled the prospective adoptive parents, who was of the same race and religion and had the same ethnic background so that the adopted child might pass as a birth child. This was consistent with the idea that adoption should mirror nature. To further illustrate that aim, as stated above, some jurisdictions by statute established a minimum age for the adoptive parents. Some required the adoptive parents to be older than the child to be adopted by a certain number of years, although in some jurisdictions that requirement is waived in kinship adoptions (adoption within a family). Secrecy was attached to adoption at that time and any discussion of a child having been adopted, even among family member,s was taboo. Indeed, some adopted children lived their entire lives not knowing that they had been adopted, only learning about the adoption in a will. That has changed with the advent of open adoption and the removal of bars to access to adoption records.

Standards for agency placement have often reflected the advancement of certain social values by emphasizing the continuity of conventional family patterns, religion, ethnicity, and race of the birth parents and the adoptive couple. Choosing conventional family patterns as a standard for placement is reflected in agencies' preference for married couples of childbearing ages over older couples or single men or women, or preferring financially secure married couples where the wife is not employed in the workforce outside of the home, to a couple of two working people. Through the years, the continuity of certain values has dominated over others, having much to do with contemporary social and even political issues. However, modern American adoption statutes express the goal of adoption as promoting a child's best interests, which also ultimately depends on a judge's discretion. Those best interests have changed over time as new family formations have evolved and are judicially recognized.

1. Religion

Matching the religion of the birth mother with that of the prospective adoptive couple was promi-

nent in adoption practice in the 1950s. The Massachusetts case of *In re Goldman*, 121 N.E.2d 843
(Mass. 1954) and the New York case of *In re Max-
well*, 151 N.E.2d 848 (N.Y. 1958) raised the importance of religion in adoption placement. At issue in
both cases was the interpretation of the phrase
"when practicable" in each state's adoption statute.
The Supreme Judicial Court of Massachusetts held
that "when practicable" should be interpreted as a
mandate to search for an adoptive couple of the
same religion of the child and only if such a couple
cannot be located can a child be placed with a
couple of a different religion. In *Goldman,* the birth
mother who gave birth to twins was Roman Catholic and the prospective adoptive parents were Jewish. The highest court in Massachusetts held that
allowing the Jewish couple to adopt Roman Catholic
children (a religion imputed to them because of the
mother) was not in the children's best interests.
The New York court interpreted "when practicable" as giving discretion to a judge, particularly
when, in that case, the mother did not embrace any
particular religion.

It should be noted that during the 1950s, and
even earlier, private adoption agencies were very
often faith-based, such as Catholic Charities and
Jewish Family Service as contrasted with secular
agencies like Family Service of America. Faith-
based agencies served their respective religious
communities, offering services to mothers who
wanted to relinquish their children for adoption and
prospective adoptive parents desiring to adopt chil-

dren. During the 1950s it would have been unusual for a couple not of the religion of the faith-based agency to apply to adopt a child relinquished to that agency.

Fifty years later, religion is a factor and is addressed in the adoption statutes of at least twelve jurisdictions. However, it is one factor among others and is not necessarily a decisive factor unless the birth mother wishes it to be so and makes those wishes known to the agency to whom she has relinquished her child or where a child has been baptized or brought into a particular faith through a formal ceremony. In the latter instances, placement of the child with adoptive parents of that faith would probably be in the child's best interests, a goal of all adoptions.

2. Race

A half-century ago, because matching included race as well as religion it would have been unusual to place an African American child with a Caucasian couple. It was thought that African American children should be raised by African American parents and that a concerted effort should be made to recruit those parents. As the number of Caucasian children available for adoption decreased during the 1980s, and the available African American children increased, transracial adoption emerged as a viable alternative to allowing those children to live in long term foster care. Transracial adoption is the placement for adoption of a child clearly identified as having been born to parents of the same race with

an individual or couple of a different race. Some
have advocated that transracial adoption should be
the last resort in the placement of a child for
adoption (the alternative being long term foster
care) not the first approach. That position, preva-
lent for years, is based on the idea that race matters
and that a child of a particular race, for example,
African American, should be placed with a couple of
the same race so that the child will not lose his
identity and his cultural heritage, both of which are
part of his very being and thus worth preserving.
Further, it is believed that transracial adoption
could potentially cause psychological complications
for the child who might find it difficult to become
acculturated in a world hostile to him because of his
race.

Those who advocate transracial adoption base
their position on the belief that although race is
important, it is not the defining placement standard. They believe that a couple of a race different
from the child who has the capacity to respect the
race of the child and provide the child with an
environment where the child can flourish as an
African American or as a Vietnamese or Chinese
can be an excellent adoptive parent. In addition,
there is a political dimension to the promotion of
transracial adoption. That is, that it is nondiscrimi-
natory and in a way can promote national harmony.
If one feels that race should not matter in defining
anyone and that ultimately a pluralistic society
should not discourage interracial relationships, like
interracial marriage, then transracial adoption

should be available if placement with an African American couple is not possible. In the United States one in seven new marriages is interracial [Black? White? Asian? More Young Americans Choose all of the Above, *The New York Times*, January 30, 2011 at 1] which illustrates the fact that interracial families may no longer be considered out of the ordinary.

Agencies often utilize transracial adoption for children who are hard to place because of their race, their age, their being a part of a sibling group or because of health issues. It is not unusual for those hard to place children to be placed with single men or women who are beyond child bearing age or same-sex couples living in a domestic partnership or a civil union.

The federal government's position on the impact of race on adoption programs funded by the government was spelled out in the Multiethnic Placement Act of 1994 (423 U.S.C.A. § 5115a (West 1994). That act permitted a state agency to consider race as a placement factor if, in conjunction with other factors the consideration of race was in the best interests of the child. The Act was replaced with a provision in the Small Business and Job Protection Act of 1996 (Pub. L. 104–188, Title 1 Sub. Tit. H. § 1808, 110 Stat. 1755, 1903 (1996)) which prohibits any agency or individual involved in adoption or foster care placement receiving federal funds to deny a child's adoptive or foster care placement on the basis of race, color or national origin. Native Americans are exempt from that provision. The adoption of Native American children is governed by the Indian Child Welfare Act of 1978, which limits placement of a child for adoption to the child's family, members of the tribe or other Native American families. (25 U.S.C. §§ 1901–63.)

3. Sexual Orientation

Before 2003 no state supreme court had decided that the restriction of a marriage license to a same-sex couple was a violation of that couple's fundamental right to marry. This changed with the decision of *Goodridge v. Department of Public Health*, 798 N.E.2d 941 (Mass. 2003) by the Supreme Judicial Court of Massachusetts. In that historic case, the highest court in Massachusetts and the oldest American state supreme court held that restricting marriage to a heterosexual couple denied the same-sex couple the "protections, benefits, and obligations conferred by civil marriage to two individuals of the same sex who wish to marry" under its state constitution. *Id.* at 948.

One of the major arguments against recognizing same-sex marriage in the *Goodridge* case related to the raising of children. To the Department of Public Health, the three legislative rationales for prohibiting same-sex couples from marrying were: "(1) Providing a 'favorable setting for procreation': (2) ensuring the optimal setting for child rearing, which the department defines as "a two-parent family with one parent of each sex' and (3) preserving scarce State and private financial resources." *Id.* at 961. A majority of the court rejected the argument

dealing with the procreation of children as a ratio-
nale for heterosexual marriage, asserting that adoption is an alternative to procreative heterosexual
intercourse. Indeed, the court stated, "While it is
certainly true that many, perhaps most, married
couples have children together (assisted or unassist-
ed), it is the exclusive and permanent commitment
of the marriage partners to one another, not the
begetting of children, that is the sine qua non of
civil marriage." *Id*.

The *Goodridge* decision did not herald a wide-
spread legal acceptance of same-sex marriage, but it
did cause legal responses. Since 2003, Connecticut,
Vermont, New Hampshire, Iowa and the District of
Columbia have legalized same-sex marriage either
by court decision or legislative action. In June 2011,
the New York State legislature enacted a law that
allows same-sex marriages to be performed in that
state. Prior to that, New York courts, like those
currently in New Jersey and Rhode Island, had
recognized same-sex marriages legally performed in
states where such marriages were legal. In 2012,
legislatures in the State of Washington, Maryland
and New Jersey passed legislation legalizing same-
sex marriage. The governor of New Jersey, however, vetoed the legislation. Internationally, same-sex
marriages are legal either by court decision or legislative action in Belgium, Canada, The Netherlands,
South Africa, Portugal, Spain, Argentina and Den-
mark.

The majority of American jurisdictions still maintain a ban on same-sex marriages. At least forty-one
states have enacted statutes or constitutional

amendments reflecting that position. Of those, twenty-nine states have constitutional amendments restricting marriage to a man and a woman. In addition, those states would not recognize same-sex marriages celebrated in another state. In 1996, Congress enacted the Defense of Marriage Act (DOMA), which has two key provisions. The first denies any federal recognition to same-sex couples married in a state that has legalized same-sex marriage, like Massachusetts. 1 U.S.C.A. § 7 (1996). The second allows a state to deny recognition of a valid same-sex marriage entered into in another American jurisdiction. 28 U.S.C.A. § 1738C (1996).

In 2010, the constitutionality of DOMA was challenged in the federal court in the Commonwealth of Massachusetts, and on July 8, 2010, the court found section 3 unconstitutional under the Equal Protection Clause. *Gill v. Office of Pers. Mgmt.*, 699 F.Supp.2d 374 (D.Mass. 2010). In the companion case, the district court accepted the Commonwealth's argument that section 3 violated the Spending Clause and the Tenth Amendment. *Massachusetts v. United States Dep't of Health & Human Servs.*, 698 F.Supp.2d 234, 249, 253 (D.Mass. 2010). In declaring section 3 unconstitutional, the district court enjoined the federal officials and agencies from enforcing that section, but the court stayed injunctive relief pending appeals.

The Court of Appeals for the First Circuit affirmed the judgment of the district court, but stayed the mandate due to a high probability that certiorari would be sought and granted. *Massachusetts v.*

United States Dep't of Health & Human Servs. et al., 682 F.3d 1 (1st Cir. 2012).

Citing *Troxel v. Granville*, 530 U.S. 57, 63 (2000), the court in *Goodridge* stated, ''The demographic changes of the past century make it difficult to speak of an average American family. The composition of families varies greatly from household to household.'' To support that statement, the court went on to cite *Adoption of Tammy*, 619 N.E.2d 315 (Mass. 1993) in which the same court approved of co-parent adoption. *Id.* at 962–63.

Single parent adoption, which is authorized by statute in at least twenty-two states, as well as the adoption of a child by a same-sex couple would be an illustration of families that do not conform to traditional family patterns. Florida and Mississippi ban adoption by a same-sex couple. FLA. STAT. ANN. § 63.042(3) (2005); MISS. CODE ANN. § 93–17–3(2) (2004). The Florida prohibition was challenged on the grounds of due process and equal protection in *Lofton v. Secretary of the Dep't of Children and Family Services*, 358 F.3d 804 (11th Cir. 2004), and the Federal Court of Appeals for the 11th Circuit rejected the claim.

It is hard to support the claim that a married same-sex couple will not be appropriate or would be inferior parents for an adopted child. Since 2004 when same-sex couples began to marry in Massachusetts, there have been no comprehensive longitudinal studies by child development experts, following an adopted newborn through adolescence and young adulthood to substantiate that claim. However, there is a substantial body of legal scholarship, citing social science research, that supports the conclusion that children adopted by same-sex couples do not suffer emotional harm because of their parents' sexual preference. The Child Welfare League of America, the major voluntary association of social services agencies, and an organization that sponsors child welfare research as well as setting standards for agency practice, has recommended that prospective adoptive parents "be assessed on the basis of their abilities to successfully parent a child needing family membership and not on their * * * differing life style or sexual orientation." Standards of Excellence for Adoption Services, Standard 4.7 (rev. ed. 2000).

In *Finstuen v. Crutcher*, 496 F.3d 1139 (10th Cir. 2007), the issue presented to the Federal Court of Appeals for the 10th Circuit was whether the Commissioner of Health for the Oklahoma State Department of Health was required to issue revised birth certificates for children born in Oklahoma but adopted in California by a same-sex couple where such an adoption was legal. Oklahoma's statute governing the recognition of parent-child relationships that are created by out-of-state adoptions had an exception to that recognition that read: "Except that, this state, any of its agencies, or any court of this state shall not recognize an adoption by more than one individual or the same sex from any other state or foreign jurisdiction. OKLA. STAT. tit. 10,

§ 7502–1.4(A) (the 'adoption amendment')." The court cited *Milwaukee County v. M.E. White Co.*, 296 U.S. 268 (1935) to explain the purpose and policies behind the Full Faith and Credit Clause:

> The very purpose of the full faith and credit clause was to alter the status of the several states as independent foreign sovereignties, each free to ignore obligations created under the laws or by the judicial proceedings of the others, and to make them integral parts of a single nation throughout which a remedy upon a just obligation might be demanded as a right, irrespective of the state of its origin.

Id. at 276–77. The court then went on to state that there was no "public policy" exception to the Full Faith and Credit Clause that could be applied to judgments, that adoption decrees were judgments that are entitled to recognition and therefore the Oklahoma adoption amendment was unconstitutional. It affirmed the lower court's decision, and ordered the issuance of revised birth certificates for the adopted children of the parents in the case who had standing to sue.

a. State Laws Regarding Gay Adoption

State	Code Provision	Permits single LGBT individuals to adopt?[2]	Permits same-sex couples to jointly adopt?	Permits same-sex second parent adoption?	Notes
Alabama	ALA. CODE § 26–10A–5	Yes. No restrictions on	Not expressly prohibit-	Not expressly prohibited	

State	Code Provision	Permits single LGBT individuals to adopt?[2]	Permits same-sex couples to jointly adopt?	Permits same-sex second parent adoption?	Notes
	(2012).	who may adopt.	ed by statute. No state court ruling on the issue.	by statute. Second parent adoptions by heterosexual couples allowed in some jurisdictions, but no state court ruling on same-sex second parent adoptions.	
Alaska	ALASKA STAT. § 25. 23.020 (2012).	Yes. No restrictions on who may adopt.	Not expressly prohibited by statute. No state court ruling on the issue.	Not expressly prohibited by statute. No state court ruling on the issue.	
Arizona	ARIZ. REV. STAT. ANN. § 8–103 (2012).	Yes. No restrictions on who may adopt.	Not expressly prohibited by statute. No state court ruling on the issue.	Not expressly prohibited by statute. No state court ruling on the issue.	
Arkansas	ARK. CODE ANN. § 9–9–204 (2011).	Yes. No restrictions on who may adopt.	Not expressly prohibited by statute. No state court ruling on the issue.	Not expressly prohibited by statute. No state court ruling on the issue.	In 2008, voters passed Act 1, which prohibited cohabiting, unmarried persons

State	Code Provision	Permits single LGBT individuals to adopt?[2]	Permits same-sex couples to jointly adopt?	Permits same-sex second parent adoption?	Notes
					from adopting or serving as foster parents. A circuit court judge recently declared the measure unconstitutional, but the state plans to appeal. *Cole v. Arkansas*, 2010 WL 6451863 (Ark. Cir. Ct. 2010).
California	CAL. FAM. CODE § 8802 (2012).	Yes. No restrictions on who may adopt.	Yes.	Yes. *Sharon S. v. Superior Court*, 73 P.3d 554 (Cal. 2003). Furthermore, registered domestic partners can use the state's stepparent adoption laws to adopt each other's children. CAL. FAM. CODE § 9000(b).

State	Code Provision	Permits single LGBT individuals to adopt?[2]	Permits same-sex couples to jointly adopt?	Permits same-sex second parent adoption?	Notes
Colorado	COLO. REV. STAT. § 19–5–202 (2012).	Yes. No restrictions on who may adopt.	Not expressly prohibited by statute. No state court ruling on the issue.	Yes. A 2007 amendment to Colo. Rev. Stat. § 19–5–203 permits second parent adoption with written consent of single parent.	
Connecticut	CONN. GEN. STAT. § 45a–726 (2012).	Yes. No restrictions on who may adopt.	Yes. No restrictions on who may adopt.	Yes. Considering Kerrigan v. Commissioner of Public Health, 957 A.2d 407 (Conn. 2008).	Sexual orientation may be considered in making placements, but it does not appear that any petitions have been denied on these grounds.
Delaware	DEL. CODE ANN. tit. 13, § 903 (2011).	Yes. No restrictions on who may adopt.	Not expressly prohibited by statute. No state court ruling on the issue.	In some jurisdictions. At least one Delaware family court has held that a same-sex partner may adopt partner's	

State	Code Provision	Permits single LGBT individuals to adopt?[2]	Permits same-sex couples to jointly adopt?	Permits same-sex second parent adoption?	Notes
				child. *In re Hart*, 806 A.2d 1179 (Del. Fam. Ct. 2001).	
District of Columbia	D.C. CODE § 16–302 (2012).	Yes. No restrictions on who may adopt.	Yes. D.C. Court of Appeals has interpreted § 16–302 as permitting any unmarried couple to adopt if in the best interests of the child. *In re M.M.D.*, 662 A.2d 837 (D.C. 1995).	Yes. *In re M.M.D.* 662 A.2d 837 (D.C. 1995).	
Florida	FLA. STAT. § 63.042 (3) (2012).	No. Explicitly prohibited by statute.	No. Explicitly prohibited by statute.	No. Explicitly prohibited by statute.	In 2008, Florida's statute was held unconstitutional by the Miami Circuit Court. *In re Adoption of Doe*, 2008 WL 5006172 (Fla. Cir. Ct. 2008). That case is currently be-

State	Code Provision	Permits single LGBT individuals to adopt?[2]	Permits same-sex couples to jointly adopt?	Permits same-sex second parent adoption?	Notes
					ing appealed.
Georgia	GA. CODE ANN. § 19–8–3 (2011).	Yes. No restrictions on who may adopt.	Not expressly prohibited by statute. No state court ruling on the issue.	Not expressly prohibited by statute. No appellate state court ruling on same-sex second parent adoptions, but some trial courts have permitted them.	
Hawaii	HAW. REV. STAT. § 578–1 (2011).	Yes. No restrictions on who may adopt.	Not expressly prohibited by statute. No state court ruling on the issue.	Not expressly prohibited by statute. No state court ruling on the issue.	
Idaho	IDAHO CODE ANN. § 16–1501 (2012).	Yes. No restrictions on who may adopt.	Not expressly prohibited by statute. No state court ruling on the issue.	Not expressly prohibited by statute. No state court ruling on the issue.	
Illinois	750 ILL. COMP. STAT. 50/2 (2011).	Yes. No restrictions on who may adopt.	Yes. *Petition of K.M.*, 653 N.E.2d 888 (Ill. App. Ct. 1995).	Yes. *Petition of K.M.*, 653 N.E.2d 888 (Ill. App. Ct. 1995).	

State	Code Provision	Permits single LGBT individuals to adopt?[2]	Permits same-sex couples to jointly adopt?	Permits same-sex second parent adoption?	Notes
Indiana	IND. CODE ANN. § 31–19 –2–2 (2011).	Yes. No restrictions on who may adopt.	Yes. *In re Infant Girl W.*, 845 N.E.2d 229 (Ind. Ct. App. 2006)	Yes. State appellate court has interpreted statute to permit same-sex second parent adoptions of partner's adopted (*In re Adoption of M.M.G.C.*, 785 N.E.2d 267 (Ind. Ct. App. 2003)) and biological child (*In re Adoption of K.S.P.*, 804 N.E.2d 1253 (Ind. Ct. App. 2004)).	
Iowa	IOWA CODE ANN. § 600.4 (2012).	Yes. No restrictions on who may adopt.	Not expressly prohibited by statute. No state court ruling on the issue.	Not expressly prohibited by statute. No state court ruling on the issue.	
Kansas	KAN. STAT. ANN. § 59– 2113	Yes. No restrictions on who may adopt.	Not expressly prohibited by statute.	Not expressly prohibited by statute. No	

State	Code Provision	Permits single LGBT individuals to adopt?[2]	Permits same-sex couples to jointly adopt?	Permits same-sex second parent adoption?	Notes
	(2012).		No state court ruling on the issue.	state court ruling on the issue.	
Kentucky	KY. REV. STAT. ANN. § 199. 470 (2011).	Yes. No restrictions on who may adopt.	Not expressly prohibited by statute. No state court ruling on the issue.	Not expressly prohibited by statute. No state court ruling on the issue.	
Louisiana	LA. CHILD CODE ANN. art. 1198 (2011).	Yes. No restrictions on who may adopt.	Not expressly prohibited by statute. No state court ruling on the issue.	Not expressly prohibited by statute. No state court ruling on the issue.	
Maine	ME. REV. STAT. ANN. tit. 18–A, § 9–301 (2011).	Yes. No restrictions on who may adopt.	Yes. *Adoption of M.A.*, 930 A.2d 1088 (Me. 2007).	Not expressly prohibited by statute. No state court ruling on the issue.	
Maryland	MD. CODE ANN. FAM. LAW §§ 5–331, 5–345 (2012).	Yes. No restrictions on who may adopt.	Not expressly prohibited by statute. No state court ruling on the issue.	Not expressly prohibited by statute. No state court ruling on the issue.	Regulations specifically prohibit denial of adoption application based on sexual orientation. MD. CODE REGS. 07.05.03. 09(A)(2)

State	Code Provision	Permits single LGBT individuals to adopt?[2]	Permits same-sex couples to jointly adopt?	Permits same-sex second parent adoption?	Notes
Massachusetts	MASS. GEN. LAWS ch. 210, § 1 (2012).	Yes. No restrictions on who may adopt.	Yes. *Adoption of Tammy*, 619 N.E.2d 315 (Mass. 1993).	Yes. *Adoption of Tammy*, 619 N.E.2d 315 (Mass. 1993).	
Michigan	MICH. COMP. LAWS ANN. § 710.24 (2012).	Yes. No restrictions on who may adopt.	No. State appellate court has ruled that only married couples may jointly adopt. *In re Adams*, 473 N.W.2d 712 (Mich. Ct. App. 1991). However, at least one lower court has permitted an unmarried same-sex couple to adopt. *Hansen v. McClellan*, 2006 WL 3524059 (Mich. Ct. App. 2006).	Maybe. No explicit prohibition. However, one judge has acted to block such adoptions.	The state attorney general has issued an opinion stating that same-sex couples legally married in other jurisdictions are not permitted to jointly adopt in Michigan. However, one member of a same-sex couple can adopt as a single person. 2004 Mich. Op. Att'y Gen. 7160.
Minnesota	MINN. STAT. ANN.	Yes. No restrictions on	Not expressly prohibit-	Not expressly prohibited	

State	Code Provision	Permits single LGBT individuals to adopt?[2]	Permits same-sex couples to jointly adopt?	Permits same-sex second parent adoption?	Notes
	§ 259.22 (2012).	who may adopt.	ed by statute. No state court ruling on the issue.	by statute. No state court ruling on the issue.	
Mississippi	MISS. CODE ANN. § 93–17 –3(4) (2011).	Yes. No restrictions on who may adopt.	No. Adoption by same-sex couples expressly prohibited by statute. MISS. CODE ANN. § 93–17– 3(5).	Maybe. Although an unmarried adult can adopt, the prohibition against joint adoption by same-sex couples arguably prevents same-sex second parent adoptions as well.	
Missouri	MO. ANN. STAT. § 453.010 (2011).	Yes. No restrictions on who may adopt.	Not expressly prohibited by statute. No state court ruling on the issue.	Not expressly prohibited by statute. No state court ruling on the issue.	
Montana	MONT. CODE ANN. § 42–1 –106 (2011).	Yes. No restrictions on who may adopt.	Not expressly prohibited by statute. No state court ruling on the issue.	Not expressly prohibited by statute. No state court ruling on the issue.	
Nebraska	NEB. REV. STAT. § 43–101	Yes. No restrictions on	Probably not. Not expressly	No. A same-sex partner	

State	Code Provision	Permits single LGBT individuals to adopt?[2]	Permits same-sex couples to jointly adopt?	Permits same-sex second parent adoption?	Notes
	(2011).	who may adopt.	prohibited by statute. No state court ruling on the issue. However, in light of the state supreme court's ruling in *In re Adoption of Luke*, joint same-sex adoptions are unlikely to be permitted.	cannot adopt a partner's child without terminating the other partner's parental rights. *In re Adoption of Luke*, 640 N.W.2d 374 (Neb. 2002).	
Nevada	NEV.REV. STAT. § 127.030 (2011).	Yes. No restrictions on who may adopt.	Not expressly prohibited by statute. No state court ruling on the issue.	Not expressly prohibited by statute. No state court ruling on the issue.	Regulations specifically prohibit denial of adoption application based on sexual orientation. NEV. ADMIN. CODE § 127.351
New Hampshire	N.H. REV. STAT. ANN. § 170–B:4 (2011).	Yes. No restrictions on who may adopt.	Probably. In 1987, the state supreme court held that two unmarried adults may not	Not expressly prohibited by statute. No state court ruling on the issue.	

State	Code Provision	Permits single LGBT individuals to adopt?[2]	Permits same-sex couples to jointly adopt?	Permits same-sex second parent adoption?	Notes
			jointly adopt. *In re Jason C.*, 533 A.2d 32 (N.H. 1987). However, several judges have apparently permitted same-sex couples to adopt. Furthermore, gay marriage is now legal in New Hampshire, so same-sex couples who are married should now be able to adopt in all jurisdictions.		
New Jersey	N.J. STAT. ANN. § 9:3–43 (2012).	Yes. No restrictions on who may adopt.	Yes. *Matter of Adoption of Two Children by H.N.R.*, 666 A.2d 535 (N.J. Super. Ct. App. Div. 1995).	Yes. *Matter of Adoption of Two Children by H.N.R.*, 666 A.2d 535 (N.J. Super. Ct. App. Div. 1995).	Regulations specifically prohibit denial of adoption application based on sexual orientation. N.J. ADMIN. CODE

State	Code Provision	Permits single LGBT individuals to adopt?[2]	Permits same-sex couples to jointly adopt?	Permits same-sex second parent adoption?	Notes
					10:121C–2.6.
New Mexico	N.M. STAT. ANN. § 32A–5–11 (2011).	Yes. No restrictions on who may adopt.	Not expressly prohibited by statute. No state court ruling on the issue.	Not expressly prohibited by statute. No state court ruling on the issue.	
New York	N.Y. DOM. REL. § 110 (2011).	Yes. No restrictions on who may adopt.	Yes. State's highest court has allowed unmarried couples to adopt. *In the Matter of Jacob*, 660 N.E.2d 397 (N.Y. 1995). Several lower courts have relied on that decision to permit same-sex couples to jointly adopt.	Yes. *In the Matter of Jacob*, 660 N.E.2d 397 (N.Y. 1995).	Regulations specifically prohibit denial of adoption application based on sexual orientation. N.Y. COMP. CODES R. & REGS. tit. 18, § 421.16 (h)(2).
North Carolina	N.C. GEN. STAT. § 48–1–103 (2011).	Yes. No restrictions on who may adopt.	No. Unmarried couples are not permitted to adopt. N.C. GEN. STAT.	Not expressly prohibited by statute. No state court ruling on the	

State	Code Provision	Permits single LGBT individuals to adopt?[2]	Permits same-sex couples to jointly adopt?	Permits same-sex second parent adoption?	Notes
			§ 48–2–301	issue.	
North Dakota	N.D. CENT. CODE § 14–15–03 (2011).	Yes. No restrictions on who may adopt.	Not expressly prohibited by statute. No state court ruling on the issue.	Not expressly prohibited by statute. No state court ruling on the issue.	State law expressly permits adoption agencies to consider "religious or moral" factors, including sexual orientation in denying a petition. N.D. CENT. CODE § 50–12–03.
Ohio	OHIO REV. CODE ANN. § 3107.03 (2011).	Yes. No restrictions on who may adopt.	Not expressly prohibited by statute. No state court ruling on the issue.	No. State appellate court has held that a parent's rights are terminated upon adoption of the child by a non-spousal partner. *In re Adoption of Doe*, 719 N.E.2d 1071 (Ohio Ct. App. 1998).	

State	Code Provision	Permits single LGBT individuals to adopt?[2]	Permits same-sex couples to jointly adopt?	Permits same-sex second parent adoption?	Notes
Oklahoma	OKLA. STAT. tit. 10, § 750 3–1.1 (2012).	Yes. No restrictions on who may adopt.	Not expressly prohibited by statute. However, one appellate court has construed the statute narrowly to hold that an unmarried couple could not jointly adopt. *In re Adoption of M.C.D.*, 42 P.3d 873 (Okla. Civ. App. 2001).	Not expressly prohibited by statute. No state court ruling on the issue.	
Oregon	OR. REV. STAT. § 109.309 (2012).	Yes. No restrictions on who may adopt.	Yes. OR. ADMIN. R. 413–120– 0200(3).	Not expressly prohibited by statute. No state court ruling on the issue.	
Pennsylvania	23 PA. CONS. STAT. § 2312 (2011).	Yes. No restrictions on who may adopt.	Not expressly prohibited by statute. One lower court granted an adoption to a	Yes. *In re Adoption of R.B.F. and R.C.F.*, 803 A.2d 1195 (Pa. 2002).	

State	Code Provision	Permits single LGBT individuals to adopt?[2]	Permits same-sex couples to jointly adopt?	Permits same-sex second parent adoption?	Notes
			same-sex couple, although it is unclear whether this was done as a joint adoption or a second parent adoption. *In re Adoption of E.O.G.*, 28 Pa. D. & C.4th 262 (Pa. Com.Pl. 1993).		
Rhode Island	R.I. GEN. LAWS § 15-7 -4(a) (2011).	Yes. No restrictions on who may adopt.	Not expressly prohibited by statute. No state court ruling on the issue.	Not expressly prohibited by statute. No state court ruling on the issue.	
South Carolina	S.C. CODE ANN. § 63- 9-60 (2012).	Yes. No restrictions on who may adopt.	Not expressly prohibited by statute. No state court ruling on the issue.	Not expressly prohibited by statute. No state court ruling on the issue.	
South Dakota	S.D. CODI- FIED LAWS § 25- 6-2 (2012).	Yes. No restrictions on who may adopt.	Not expressly prohibited by statute. No state court rul-	Not expressly prohibited by statute. No state court rul-	

State	Code Provision	Permits single LGBT individuals to adopt?[2]	Permits same-sex couples to jointly adopt?	Permits same-sex second parent adoption?	Notes
			ing on the issue.	ing on the issue.	
Tennessee	TENN. CODE ANN. § 36–1 –115 (2012).	Yes. No restrictions on who may adopt.	Not expressly prohibited by statute. No state court ruling on the issue.	Not expressly prohibited by statute. No state court ruling on the issue.	State appellate court has held that sexual orientation may be considered in the "best interests" analysis, but cannot be controlling. *In re Adoption of M.J.S.*, 44 S.W.3d 41 (Tenn. Ct. App. 2000).
Texas	TEX. FAMILY CODE ANN. § 162. 001 (2011).	Yes. No restrictions on who may adopt.	Not expressly prohibited by statute. State appellate court has upheld such adoptions, but made no substantive decision on whether same-sex couples can jointly peti	Not expressly prohibited by statute. State appellate court has upheld such adoptions but made no substantive decision on permissibility of same-sex second parent adoptions. *Hobbs v.*	

State	Code Provision	Permits single LGBT individuals to adopt?[2]	Permits same-sex couples to jointly adopt?	Permits same-sex second parent adoption?	Notes
			tion. *Goodson v. Castellanos*, 214 S.W.3d 741 (Tex. App. 2007).	*Van Stavern*, 249 S.W.3d 1 (Tex. App. 2006).	
Utah	UTAH CODE ANN. § 78B–6 –117 (2011).	Yes. However, unmarried, co-habiting couples are prohibited from adopting.	No. Un-married, cohabiting couples are prohibited from adopting.	No. Un-married, cohabiting couples are prohibited from adopting.	
Vermont	VT. STAT. ANN. tit. 15A, § 1– 102 (2012).	Yes. No restrictions on who may adopt.	Yes.	Yes. VT. STAT. ANN. tit. 15A, § 1– 102(b).	
Virginia	VA. CODE ANN. § 63.2 –1201 (2012).	Yes. No restrictions on who may adopt.	Not ex-pressly prohibited by statute. No state court ruling on the issue.	Not ex-pressly prohibited by stat-ute. No state court ruling on the issue.	
Washington	WASH. REV. CODE § 23.33. 140 (2012).	Yes. No restrictions on who may adopt.	Not ex-pressly prohibited by statute. No state court ruling on the issue.	Not ex-pressly prohibited by stat-ute. No state court ruling on the issue.	
West Virginia	W. VA. CODE § 48–22 –201 (2012).	Yes. No restrictions on who may adopt.	Not ex-pressly prohibited by statute.	Not ex-pressly prohibited by stat-ute. No	

State	Code Provision	Permits single LGBT individuals to adopt?[2]	Permits same-sex couples to jointly adopt?	Permits same-sex second parent adoption?	Notes
			No state court ruling on the issue.	state court ruling on the issue.	
Wisconsin	Wis. Stat. § 48.82 (2011).	Yes. No restrictions on who may adopt.	Probably not. However, courts have strongly suggested that same-sex joint adoptions are not available. *See, e.g., In re Custody of H.S.H.–K.*, 533 N.W.2d 419 n.41 (Wis. 1995).	No. A same-sex partner cannot adopt a partner's child without terminating the other partner's parental rights. *In Interest of Angel Lace M.*, 516 N.W.2d 678 (Wis. 1994).	
Wyoming	Wyo. Stat. Ann. § 1–22–103 (2011).	Yes. No restrictions on who may adopt.	Not expressly prohibited by statute. No state court ruling on the issue.	Not expressly prohibited by statute. No state court ruling on the issue.	

[2] Age and residency requirements not considered.

PART TWO
MAINTAINING THE ADOPTIVE RELATIONSHIP

The goal of a successful adoption placement is the full integration of the child into the adoptive family. The ideal is that the adopted child should feel "as if" he or she were the natural child of her parents and treated as such. If he or she enters a family where there are natural or adopted children already, they would be her siblings. If an adopted child lives with and is raised together with her adopted siblings, especially from infancy, it would seem to follow that in those situations, an adopted child should not be allowed to marry her adopted siblings even though they are not blood relatives. To do so would be considered an incestuous relationship. Indeed a lower Pennsylvania court held that adoption imposes on an adopted child a relationship comparable to one by consanguinity and therefore the child in the case could not marry his adopted sister. *In re MEW and MLB*, 4 Pa. D. & C.3d 51 (Pa.Com.Pl. 1977). That result would probably be reached in a great majority of the states.

For example, the Colorado statutes reads: "*Prohibited marriages*. (1) The following marriages are prohibited: ... (b) A marriage between an ancestor and a descendant or between a brother and sister, whether the relationship is by the half or the whole blood or by adoption ..." However, in *Israel v. Allen*, 577 P.2d 762 (Colo. 1978), the Colorado Supreme Court held that that provision was unconstitutional as a violation of the Equal Protection Clause of the Fourteenth Amendment to the United States Constitution. In that case the court held that there was no rational basis for denying the adoptive siblings in the case the right to marry since they had not been raised together, having been adopted as teenagers and had actually known each other for a few years before they decided to marry.

For many decades in American adoption laws and practices, the adoption decree terminated the child's legal relationships with his or her birth family. In some instances and in some states, there might be inheritance rights that might survive the adoption, like an adopted child being able to inherit from his or her birth parents but not through them and the birth parents being able to inherit from the adopted child. Generally speaking, however, the decree ended any personal contacts. This is not to say that terminating legal relationships also cuts off emotional ties, because it may not. Some child development specialists maintain that the bond between the newborn and birth mother is so important that it remains throughout life even if not on a conscious level.

Believing that integrating the adopted child into his or her adoptive family requires that there be no contact between the adopted child and his or her birth family, adoption specialists for years have advocated a clean break. To them such a break is beneficial both to the adoptive family who can fully incorporate the child into their family and the birth mother who can accept the finality of the relinquishment and resume her life with the knowledge that her child is secure in a new home. Adoptive parents may be reluctant to accept the birth mother's involvement in their family, feeling a sense of being observed or scrutinized by her. Such involvement may even prompt competition between the birth mother and the adoptive parents. All of these feelings would have a negative impact on the adoptive parents and their attempt to have a normal relationship with their adopted child.

The model of adoption that includes full termination of the rights of the birth parents and a cloak of secrecy over the identity of the birth parents has changed in some states. The new model of adoption breaks from the past in its allowing contact between birth parents and the adopted child and the ability of the adopted child to know the identity of his or her birth parents

I. Post Adoption Decree Contacts

Lawyers are often law-makers although they are usually not considered as functioning in that role. Post-adoption decree contacts between the birth mother and the adoptive parents arose in part from negotiations between the lawyer for the social service agency and the birth mother during litigation as a strategy for avoiding an appeal. For example, where a termination of parental rights case was being appealed by the birth mother and the social service agency lawyer felt that the appeal had merit, the price for not appealing the termination order might be a negotiated settlement whereby the birth mother would not appeal if she and perhaps her parents could have some limited access to her child who was to be adopted. The settlement then included a judicially approved contract in which the parties agreed to a visitation schedule. The judicial authority to approve such a written contract was derived from the ability of the judge to utilize his or her discretion in advancing the best interests of a child, a basic principle in child custody cases, especially those involving termination of parental rights and adoption.

A post-adoption decree contact may be the appropriate outcome for situations involving a child over the age of five who has had contact and a positive relationship with his or her birth parents while in foster care and continuation of that contact after adoption is in the child's best interests. In California, Indiana and Massachusetts where a child's consent to his or her adoption is allowed, a post-adoption contact may be a provision suggested by the child himself. [See CAL. FAM. CODE § 8616.5(d); IND. CODE ANN. § 31–19–16–2(6); MASS. GEN. LAWS ANN. ch. 210 § 6C(c)]. An adoption decree that allows post-adoption contacts has been called "open adoption."

II. Open Adoption

Post-adoption contacts between the adopted child and the birth parents, and in some instances birth relatives like grandparents and siblings are allowed in twenty-three states: Alaska, Arizona, California, Connecticut, Florida, Indiana, Louisiana, Maryland, Massachusetts, Minnesota, Montana, Nebraska, Nevada, New Hampshire, New Mexico, New York, Oklahoma, Oregon, Rhode Island, Texas, Vermont, Washington and West Virginia. North Carolina, Ohio, South Carolina and South Dakota have statutory provisions expressly stating that such contracts are non-binding and unenforceable. Missouri and Tennessee leave contact and visitation opportunities to the sole discretion of the adoptive parents. In Colorado, a court does not have the authority to enter a post-adoption visitation order.

In states that allow for post-adoption contact, parties are required to file the post adoption contact agreement with the court, which will incorporate the agreement into the final adoption decree. Ultimately, judicial decisions about maintaining contact between the adopted child and his or her birth parents, foster parents, relatives, like grandparents, aunts, uncles and siblings are based on the promotion of the best interests of the child. Usually, that decision follows an examination of the bonds that have been established between the adopted child and the relatives. Siblings present a special problem. Although it is often desirable to place siblings together, that is not always possible, and siblings may be separated, often causing a permanent separation. Sibling contact, then, provides one way in which the bond may be continued. Recognizing the importance of preserving sibling relationships, some jurisdictions like Indiana, Louisiana, Maryland, Massachusetts and Oklahoma make specific reference to sibling visitation in their statutes. See IND. CODE ANN. § 31–19–16.5–1 to 5–7 (West 2011); LA. CHILD. CODE ANN. art. 1269.2 (2011); MD. CODE ANN., FAM. LAW § 5–525.2 (West 2012); OKLA. STAT. ANN. tit. 10A, § 1–4–203(6) (West 2012).

In 2008 Massachusetts amended its law to read:

Any child who has attained the age of 12 years, may request visitation rights with siblings who have been separated and placed in care or have been adopted in a foster or adoptive home other than where the child resides.

MASS. GEN. LAWS ANN. ch. 119, § 26B (West 2012).

III. Post–Adoption Agreements

Post-adoption agreements may define the contacts in terms of when they can occur and the extent of the contact. In addition, it would not be unusual for post adoption agreements to be subject to a certain time frame or conditions. For example, the agreement could end when the adopted child reaches the age of majority, or the agreement could state that if the birth parent did not exercise her visitation rights for a certain period of time, the rights would cease and the agreement would be terminated. At the same time, since post-adoption agreements are contracts, if allowed in the state, they can be subject to modification, for example if there are changed or exceptional circumstances. In some states the parties are required to participate in mediation before a petition for modification may be brought to court.

A.   Post–Adoption Contact Statutes

State & Statute	What May/ Must Be Included in Post adoption Contract Agreements	Who May/ Must Be a Party	Court Approval	Legal Enforceability	Termination/ Modification
Alaska ALASKA STAT. §§ 25.23.130 (c), 180(j), (k), (l) (2012).	Nothing prohibits visitation between adoptee and birth parent(s).	The adoptee, the adoptive parent(s) and the birth parent(s) or other relatives.	To be approved, contact must be stated with specificity in writing, and done not less than 10 days after relinquishment is signed.	Upon a showing of good cause, a parent may request a hearing to seek enforcement. Failure to comply is not grounds for setting aside the adoption.	Parties may request review hearing upon showing of good cause to seek termination or modification. Court may modify, enforce, or vacate the privilege if to do so would, by clear and convincing evidence, be in the best interests of the child.
Arizona ARIZ. REV. STAT. ANN. § 8–116.01	Must state that adoptive parent(s)	Agreement must be approved	Court must find that contact is in	Agreement may be enforce-	Court may order a modification of an agree-

State & Statute	What May/ Must Be Included in Post adoption Contract Agreements	Who May/ Must Be a Party	Court Approval	Legal Enforceability	Termination/ Modification
(2012).	can terminate if he or she believes it is the best interest of the child. Must contain provisions regarding the adoption being irrevocable, and the continuing jurisdiction of the court to enforce and modify the agreement. *See* ARIZ. REV. STAT. ANN. § 8–116.01(J)	by prospective adoptive parent(s), any birth parent(s) with whom the agreement is being made, and if child is in custody of an agency, a representative of the agency.	best interests of child. Court may consider the wishes of a child who is at least 12 years old.	able even if it does not disclose identity of the parties to the agreement. Enforcement must take into account best interests of child.	ment if modification is necessary to serve the best interests of the adopted child and one of the following is true: (1) modification is agreed to by adoptive parent(s), or (2) exceptional circumstances have arisen since the agreement was approved that justify modification of the agreement. Adoptive parent(s) can terminate if they believe it is the best interest of the child.
California CA. FAM. CODE § 8616.5 (2012); CA. WELF. & INST. CODE § 366.29 (2012).	Terms of agreement are limited to, but need not include, all of the following: (a) visita-	The following persons may be parties: (a) the adopting parent(s); (b) the birth par-	Court must approve the agreement based on the best interest of the child	Court may not order compliance with agreement absent finding that party	A contact agreement may be terminated or modified only in two instances: if (1) all parties, including the child

State & Statute	What May/ Must Be Included in Post adoption Contract Agreements	Who May/ Must Be a Party	Court Approval	Legal Enforce-ability	Termi-nation/ Modification
	tion and future contact, between adoptee and the birth parent(s), and other birth relative(s); (c) provisions for sharing information about adoptee in the future. Agreement must contain warnings that failure to follow terms of agreement will not affect custody or validity of decree. *See* CA. WELF. & INST. CODE § 366.29 (e) (1), (2) & (3).	ent(s) and birth relative(s); (c) the child; and (d) in cases governed by the Indian Child Welfare Act, the adoptee's Indian Tribe.	standard.	seeking enforcement participated, or attempted to participate, in good faith appropriate dispute negotiation proceedings regarding the conflict, prior to the filing of the enforcement action. Court may not award monetary damages.	if he or she is 12 or older, have agreed in writing; or (2) the court finds it is in the bests interests of the child, there has been a substantial change in circumstances, and the party seeking the termination or modification has participated or attempted to participate in good faith alternate dispute resolution proceedings.
Connecticut CONN. GEN. STAT.	Agreements must con-	Any birth parent(s) seeking	An agreement may be	Enforce-able so long as	The court may order the arrange-

State & Statute	What May/ Must Be Included in Post adoption Contract Agreements	Who May/ Must Be a Party	Court Approval	Legal Enforceability	Termination/ Modification
§§ 45a–715(h), (i), (j), (k), (m), (n) (Supp. 2012).	tain provisions regarding the adoption being irrevocable, and birth parent(s) rights of enforcement. See CONN. GEN. STAT. §§ 45a–715(j). Permissible provisions include: provision for communication between child and birth parent(s), provision for future contact between child and/or adoptive parent(s) and birth parent(s), and a provision for the maintenance of birth par-	contact and any intended adoptive parent(s) must be parties. Counsel for the child and any guardian *ad litem* may be heard on the proposed agreement. Child must give consent if he or she is over 12.	approved by the court if: (a) each intended adoptive parent consents; (b) the intended adoptive parent(s) and birth parent(s) execute an agreement and file it with the court; (c) consent is obtained from the child if he or she is 12 or older. If court determines contact is in the best interest of the child, the court will say so, ordering the nature and frequency of contact.	agreement had been approved by all parties and agreement was filed with the court. Failure to comply is not grounds for setting aside the adoption. Before court will enforce, the parties must have participated, or attempted to participate, in good faith in mediation or other appropriate dispute resolution proceedings.	ment modified or terminated— upon motion by an adoptive parent, guardian *ad litem*, or *sua sponte*—if it believes it is in the best interests of the child. Before the motion is brought to the court the parties must participate, or attempt to participate in good faith mediation.

State & Statute	What May/ Must Be Included in Post adoption Contract Agreements	Who May/ Must Be a Party	Court Approval	Legal Enforceability	Termination/ Modification
	ent(s) medical history.				
District of Columbia D.C. Code § 4–361 (2012).	Contact, not specifically described statutorily.	Prospective adoptive parent(s) and birth parent(s). Adoptee over 14 must consent. Agreement is at sole discretion of adoptive parent(s).	Not statutorily described.	Enforcement is based upon best interests of the child standard. Before court will handle a dispute, moving party needs to show mediation or an attempt to mediate. Failure to comply is not grounds for setting aside the adoption.	Party seeking to modify or vacate order has burden to show it is in the best interests of the child.
Florida FLA. STAT. § 63.0427 (2012).	Agreement may include, but not limited to visits, written correspondence, or telephone calls.	Adoptive parent(s) and birth parent(s).	The court will determine whether contact is in the best interest of the child. In doing so, the court must con-	Not addressed statutorily.	The court may modify or terminate the agreement on the petition of the adoptive parent(s) if it believes it is in the best interests of the child. The court

State & Statute	What May/ Must Be Included in Post adoption Contract Agreements	Who May/ Must Be a Party	Court Approval	Legal Enforceability	Termination/ Modification
			sider: (a) recommendations of state agencies, foster parent(s) and/or a guardian *ad litem*; (b) statements of prospective adoptive parent(s); (c) any other information deemed relevant and material.		may order the parties to engage in mediation before hearing such a petition.
Indiana IND. CODE §§ 31–19–16–1—4, 9; 31–19–16.5–1, 2, 4, 5 (2011).	Agreements must contain provisions regarding the adoption being irrevocable, and birth parent(s) rights of enforcement. *See* IND. CODE § 31–19–16–3	The adoptive parent(s) and the birth parent(s).	A court may grant post adoption contact privileges if it finds: it is in the best interests of the child along with 6 other factors. *See* IND. CODE §§ 31–19–16–2.	Birth or adoptive parent(s), or guardian *ad litem*, or the adopted child may petition the court to compel compliance with such an agreement. Contact agreement	Upon motion from a birth or adoptive parent(s), guardian *ad litem*, or the adopted child the court may void or modify an agreement if it determines, after a hearing, that it is in the best interests of the child.

State & Statute	What May/Must Be Included in Post adoption Contract Agreements	Who May/Must Be a Party	Court Approval	Legal Enforceability	Termination/ Modification
			Court approval not necessary for agreement for a child under 2 that doesn't include visitation.	made without court approval, for child under 2 is not enforceable.	
Louisiana LA. CHILD. CODE ANN. arts. §§ 1264, 1269.1–7 (2011).	May include all types of contact and exchanges of information. Agreements must contain provisions regarding the adoption being irrevocable, and birth parent(s) rights of enforcement. *See* LA. CH.C. Arts. 1269.3 (E)	Adoptive parent(s), birth parent(s), as well as other biological relatives. Court may appoint independent counsel for child.	Court must find the agreement to be within the best interests of the child. Child must be consulted if 12 or older. If the court denies approval it shall make specific findings of fact based on suggested statutory factors. *See* LA. CH.C. Arts. 1269.5	Agreements approved by the court are enforceable. Failure to comply is not grounds for setting aside the adoption.	The court shall order continuing compliance in accordance with the agreement and refuse to modify or terminate unless it finds there has been a change of circumstances such that it is no longer in the best interests of the child. If the child is 12 or older the court shall consider his or her wishes. Before hearing a petition the court shall order

State & Statute	What May/ Must Be Included in Post adoption Contract Agreements	Who May/ Must Be a Party	Court Approval	Legal Enforceability	Termination/ Modification
					the parties to mediate.
Maryland MD. CODE ANN., FAM. LAW §§ 5–308, 525.2 (2012).	May enter into a written agreement to allow contact after the adoption, while the adopted person is a minor.	The adoptive parent(s) and the birth parent(s), though contact may be granted with a relative not a party to the agreement.	The court issues an appropriate visitation decree based on the best interests of the child.	A court will enforce such an agreement unless enforcement is not in the child's best interests. Failure to comply is not grounds for setting aside the adoption.	Either party may move the court to modify the agreement. If the court finds it is in the best interests of the child because an exceptional circumstance has arisen, the court may modify the agreement.
Massachusetts MASS. GEN. LAWS ch. 210, §§ 6C, 6D (2012).	The agreement must be made prior to the adoption decree and contain four statutorily defined statements. See MASS. GEN. LAWS ch. 210, §§ 6C (c) (1)–(3)	The adoptive parent(s) the birth parent(s) and the child if he or she is above age twelve. If the child is in custody of the Department of Children and Families, a repre-	The court approves the agreement if it finds it is in the best interests of the child, the terms are fair and reasonable, and it has been entered into knowingly and voluntari-	Yes, a party may seek to enforce by commencing a civil action for specific performance. Agreement not enforceable after the child reaches age 18. Attor-	The court may modify the agreement if it finds there has been a material and substantial change in circumstances and the modification is necessary to the best interests of the child. A court imposed modi-

State & Statute	What May/ Must Be Included in Post adoption Contract Agreements	Who May/ Must Be a Party	Court Approval	Legal Enforce- ability	Termi- nation/ Modification
		sentative of the agency and inde- pendent counsel of the child must ap- prove.	ly.	ney's fees are avail- able to the pre- vailing party if an action to enforce is wholly insub- stantial, frivolous, and not in good faith.	fication can only limit or decrease contact, can- not expand or increase amount of contact.
Minnesota MINN. STAT. § 259.58 (2012).	The agree- ment may re- gard communi- cation, contact, or visita- tion with or be- tween an adopted minor, adoptive parent(s), birth par- ents(s) and a birth rel- ative(s) or foster parent(s).	An agree- ment may be entered into be- tween: (a) adoptive parent(s) and a birth par- ent (s); (b) adop- tive par- ent(s) and any other birth rel- ative or foster parent with whom the child re- sided be- fore being adopted; or (c) adoptive parent(s)	The court may issue an order granting such con- tact, so long as it is applied for before a decree of adop- tion is granted and is- sued be- fore the issuing of such a decree or within thirty days of being ap- plied for, whichev- er is ear- lier. Agree- ment	So long as the agree- ment's terms are contained in a court order it is enforce- able. Fail- ure to comply is not grounds for set- ting aside the adop- tion. In order to move the court to enforce such an agree- ment, however, the par- ties must sign affi-	The court shall not modify an agreement unless it finds that the modifica- tion is neces- sary to serve the best in- terests of the child, and: (a) the modification is agreed to by the par- ties to the agreement, or (b) excep- tional cir- cumstances have arisen since the agreement order was entered that justify modi- fication.

State & Statute	What May/ Must Be Included in Post adoption Contract Agree- ments	Who May/ Must Be a Par- ty	Court Approval	Legal Enforce- ability	Termi- nation/ Modification
	and any other birth rel- ative if the child is adopted by a birth relative upon the death of both par- ents.		must be approved by all parties. Court must find the agree- ment to be in the best in- terest of the child.	davits in- dicating that they have me- diated or attempt- ed to me- diate the dispute.	
Missouri Mo. Rev. Stat. § 453.080 (4) (2011).	Upon comple- tion of adoption, further contact among the par- ties shall be at the discretion of the adoptive parent(s).	The par- ties to the adop- tion.	The court does not have ju- risdiction to deny further contact between the adopted person and his or her birth par- ent(s).	Not ad- dressed statutori- ly.	Not ad- dressed stat- utorily.
Montana Mont. Code Ann. § 42– 5–301 (2011).	Not stat- utorily limited, though any con- tact must be stated expressly in the agree- ment.	The birth parent(s) and the prospec- tive adop- tive par- ent(s).	The court does not approve the agree- ments and fail- ure to perform the terms of an agree- ment is not grounds for set- ting aside	Court will gen- erally en- force un- less it finds that: (a) enforce- ment is detrimen- tal to the child; (b) enforce- ment un- dermines the adop-	Not ad- dressed stat- utorily.

State & Statute	What May/ Must Be Included in Post adoption Contract Agree-ments	Who May/ Must Be a Par-ty	Court Approval	Legal Enforce-ability	Termi-nation/ Modification
			and adop-tion de-cree.	tive par-ent's pa-rental authori-ty; or (c) due to a change in circum-stances, compli-ance would be unduly burden-some to one or more of the par-ties.	
Nebraska NEB. REV. STAT. §§ 43–156 to 165 (2011).	Agree-ments are nego-tiated through a state agency and are two-year, renewa-ble obli-gations. The con-tact per-mitted may in-clude let-ters or photo-graphs sent by the adop-tive par-ent(s) to the birth	If the prospec-tive adop-tee is in the custo-dy of the Depart-ment of Health and Hu-man Ser-vices, the adoptive parent(s) and the birth par-ent(s) may en-ter into an agree-ment re-garding communi-cation or contact	The agree-ment must be approved by the court. The court may do so if it de-termines it is in the best interests of the child af-ter hear-ing from a guard-ian *ad li-tem* and being shown a written agree-	An agree-ment ap-proved by the court may be enforced by a civil action, and the prevailing party may be awarded reason-able at-torney's fees. Fail-ure to comply is not grounds for set-ting aside the adop-tion.	The court shall not modify an agreement unless it finds that the modifica-tion is neces-sary to serve the best in-terests of the child, and: (a) the modification is agreed to by the par-ties to the agreement, or (b) excep-tional cir-cumstances have arisen since

State & Statute	What May/ Must Be Included in Post adoption Contract Agreements	Who May/ Must Be a Party	Court Approval	Legal Enforceability	Termination/ Modification
	parent(s) at specified intervals providing information regarding the child's development. The statute neither precludes nor allows visitation.	after the adoption between or among the prospective adoptee and his or her birth parent(s).	ment.		
Nevada Nev. Rev. Stat. § .187 to .189.5 (2011).	No limit on what the agreement may contain, though it must be expressly written.	The natural parent(s) and the prospective adoptive parent(s).	If the court determines that the prospective adoptive parent(s) and the natural parent(s) have entered into an agreement that provides for postadoptive contact, the court shall order the prospective adoptive par-	Any action to enforce the terms of an agreement must be commenced not later than 120 days after the date the agreement was breached. Failure to comply is not grounds for setting aside the adoption.	Agreement, can only be modified or terminated by petitioning the court. Court will modify or terminate, only if (a) both parties consent, and (b) adoptive parent(s) must show: (1) a change in circumstances, and (2) the agreement is no longer in the best interests of the child.

State & Statute	What May/ Must Be Included in Post adoption Contract Agreements	Who May/ Must Be a Party	Court Approval	Legal Enforce- ability	Termi- nation/ Modification
			ent(s) to provide a copy of the agreement to the court and incorporate the agreement into the order or decree of adoption.		Modification can only limit or decrease contact, not increase or expand it.
New Hampshire N.H. REV. STAT. ANN. § 170–B:14 (2011).	An agreement must contain four statutory statements. *See* N.H. REV. STAT. ANN. § 170–B:14 (II)(e)(1)–(4). It must also include affidavits from all parties affirmatively stating the agreement was entered into knowingly and voluntarily and is	The adoptive and birth parent(s) and the Department of Health and Human Services may voluntarily participate in a court ordered mediation program to reach a voluntary agreement. Others may participate in the mediation, but cannot be parties to	The court shall approve the voluntarily mediated agreement if it is in the best interests of the child after considering a number of suggested factors. *See* N.H. REV. STAT. ANN. § 170–B:14 (II)(d)(1) (A)–(H)	Enforceable up to the child's eighteenth birthday. Failure to comply is not grounds for setting aside the adoption.	After demonstrating that they have participated or attempted in good faith to participate in mediation, the parties may request that the court modify or terminate the agreement. The court may also do this on its own if it feels it is in the best interests of the child. A modification may not, however, increase the contact or place a

State & Statute	What May/ Must Be Included in Post adoption Contract Agreements	Who May/ Must Be a Party	Court Approval	Legal Enforce-ability	Termi-nation/ Modification
	not the product of coercion, fraud, or duress. If child is 14 or older, need his or her consent.	the agreement.			greater burden on the adoptive parent(s).
New Mexico N.M. STAT. § 32A–5–35 (2011).	The contact may include exchange of identifying information or visitation between adoptee and birth relative(s). Must include two statutory disclaimers. See N.M. STAT. § 32A–5–35 (D)	The adoptive and birth parent(s) and the relatives of the birth parent(s). Court may appoint a guardian *ad litem* or attorney for the child and shall consider the wishes of the child.	The court may approve the agreement if it is in the best interests of the child. Court may consider wishes of the child, though such wishes shall not control the court.	The court has continuing jurisdiction to enforce the agreement upon motion. Failure to comply is not grounds for setting aside the adoption.	The court shall not grant a request to modify the agreement unless the moving party establishes that there has been a change in circumstances and the agreement is no longer in the child's best interests.
New York N.Y. SOC. SERV. LAW § 383–c(2)(b) (2011); N.Y. DOM. REL. LAW § 112–b (2011).	The agreement may provide for communication or contact between the adop-	The adoptive person(s), the child's birth parent(s), the authorized agency	If the court finds that the agreement is in the best interests of the child, is written	May be enforced by any party to the agreement or the adoptee's attorney by filing a	Not addressed statutorily.

State & Statute	What May/Must Be Included in Post adoption Contract Agreements	Who May/Must Be a Party	Court Approval	Legal Enforceability	Termination/Modification
	tee and birth parent(s) on such terms agreed to by the parties. Agreement may also provide for contact or communications with the adoptee's biological siblings or half-siblings.	having care and custody of the child, and the child's legal guardian as well as the child's biological siblings age fourteen or older may be parties.	and agreed to by the parties, including the child's guardian, it shall approve the agreement.	petition. Failure to comply by adoptive parent(s), not grounds to vacate adoption decree. Court will enforce agreement if in the best interests of the child.	
North Carolina N.C. GEN. STAT. § 48–3–610 (2011).	The agreements are not enforceable.	The person executing consent and the prospective adoptive parent(s).	Not addressed statutorily.	The agreement itself shall not be enforceable.	Not addressed statutorily.
Ohio OHIO REV. CODE ANN. §§ 3107.63, .65 (2011).	An open adoption may provide for the exchange of any information, including identifying information, and have	The birth and adoptive parent(s).	A probate court may refuse to approve a proposed placement or to issue a final decree of adoption if it finds	An open adoption is not enforceable.	The terms of an open adoption are voluntary and any person who has entered into one may withdraw at any time.

State & Statute	What May/ Must Be Included in Post adoption Contract Agreements	Who May/ Must Be a Party	Court Approval	Legal Enforceability	Termination/ Modification
	any other terms. There are five specific statutory provisions that state what an open adoption cannot do. See OHIO REV. CODE ANN. § 3107.65 (A) (1)–(5)		that a contact agreement has been entered into that violates the law or is not in the best interests of the child.		
Oklahoma OKLA. STAT. tit. 10, § 7505–1.5 (2012).	The agreement may provide for communication or visitation, or contact between the child, adoptive parent(s), and birth relative(s) that the child resided with before being adopted.	The adoptive parent(s) and any birth relatives by blood or marriage. For Indian children, birth relatives include those provided in the Indian Child Welfare Act.	The court may enter an order if it finds it would be in the child's best interests and poses no threat to the safety of the child or integrity of the adoptive placement.	The parties may move the court for enforcement and may be awarded reasonable attorney's fees if they succeed, however, enforcement shall not be grounds for setting aside an adoption de-	Upon motion to the court modification or termination may be approved by the court if it is in the best interests of the child and is either (a) agreed to by the birth and adoptive parent(s), or (b) exceptional circumstances have arisen to justify modification or termi-

State & Statute	What May/ Must Be Included in Post adoption Contract Agreements	Who May/ Must Be a Party	Court Approval	Legal Enforceability	Termination/ Modification
				cree, or indirect contempt of court. Parties must have mediated, or attempted to mediate the dispute.	nation. Parties must have mediated, or attempted to mediate the dispute.
Oregon OR. REV. STAT. §§ 109.119; 109.305 (2012).	An agreement may permit continuing contact between the birth relative(s) and the child or adoptive parent(s).	The adoptive and birth parent(s), birth relative(s) (that meets the requirements of ORS 109.119) and the child if he or she is at least 14 years of age.	The written agreement must be approved by the court and may be incorporated by reference in the court's approval of the adoption decree.	An agreement may be enforced by a civil action, but a court must require a showing that the parties participated or attempted in good faith to participate in mediation first. Failure to comply is not grounds for setting aside the adoption.	The court may modify the agreement if it finds that it is in the best interests of the child, the parties have participated or attempted in good faith to participate in mediation, and (a) the modification is agreed to by all original parties; or (b) exceptional circumstances have arisen to justify modification.
Rhode Island R.I.	Post-adoption	The adoptive	The court may ap-	Either birth or	The court may void or

State & Statute	What May/Must Be Included in Post adoption Contract Agreements	Who May/Must Be a Party	Court Approval	Legal Enforceability	Termination/Modification
GEN. LAWS § 15–7–14.1 (2011).	privileges may include visitation, contact, and/or conveyance of information. Agreements must contain provisions regarding the adoption being irrevocable, and birth parent(s) rights of enforcement. *See* R.I. GEN. LAWS § 15–7–14.1 (c)(1) & (2)	and birth parent(s). A child, age 12 or older, must consent.	prove such an agreement provided that it finds it is in the best interests of the child, the court finds a significant emotional attachment between the child and the birth parent(s), as well as other factors. *See* R.I. GEN. LAWS § 15–7–14.1 (b)(1)–(6)	adoptive parent(s) may file a petition with the court seeking enforcement. No monetary damages may be awarded nor does an enforcement action affect an adoption decree.	modify a post-adoption privilegement at any time if the court determines after a hearing that the best interests of the child demand it. Before such a hearing notice must be given to the adoption agency or a guardian *ad litem*.
South Carolina S.C. CODE ANN. § 63–9–760 (D) (2012).	An agreement may concern visitation, exchange of information, or other interaction between the child and	Adoptive and biological parent(s).	Not addressed statutorily.	Not enforceable and does not preserve any parental rights for the biological parent(s).	Not addressed statutorily.

State & Statute	What May/ Must Be Included in Post adoption Contract Agreements	Who May/ Must Be a Party	Court Approval	Legal Enforceability	Termination/ Modification
	any other person.				
South Dakota S.D. CODIFIED LAWS § 25–6–17 (2012).	No rights of visitation or contact unless adoptive parent(s) consents and the party is a presently married step parent, or there is a written pre-adoption agreement between birth parent(s) and adoptive parent(s).	The natural parent(s), adoptive parent(s) and a step parent.	Not addressed statutorily.	Not addressed statutorily.	Not addressed statutorily.
Tennessee TENN. CODE ANN. § 36–1–121 (f) (2012).	Any agreements are void. Statute does not prohibit an open adoption.	The adoptive parent(s) have the sole discretion to permit the parent or guardian of the child, or the siblings or other persons re-	Court cannot order visitation.	No enforceable rights.	Adoptive parent(s) can restrict any voluntary visitation or contact at their discretion.

State & Statute	What May/ Must Be Included in Post adoption Contract Agreements	Who May/ Must Be a Party	Court Approval	Legal Enforceability	Termination/ Modification
		lated to the child.			
Texas TEX. FAM. CODE ANN. §§ 161 .2061, .2062 (2011).	Agreement may allow birth parent(s) to receive specified information regarding the child; provide written communications to the child; and/or have limited access to the child.	Contact must be agreed upon by biological parent(s) and the Department of Protective and Regulatory Services.	The court may order such contact if it finds it is in the best interests of the child.	Agreement can be enforced, only if the party seeking enforcement pleads and proves, that before filing the motion for enforcement, the party attempted in good faith to resolve the dispute through mediation.	Terms may not be modified, only terminated.
Vermont VT. STAT. ANN. tit. 15A, §§ 1–109, 4–112 (2012).	May permit any a stepparent to visit or communicate with the minor after the decree of adoption becomes final. All other	The step parent, the adopted parent(s), the child if age fourteen or older, and an authorized employee of the adop-	The court may enter an order approving an agreement if it finds it is in the best interests of the child based on a 6 factor	Agreements are unenforceable for non-stepparent adoptions once the adoption is final. An agreement in a stepparent	An agreement may not be modified unless the court finds it is in the best interests of the child and: (a) the persons subject to the order request the

State & Statute	What May/ Must Be Included in Post adoption Contract Agreements	Who May/ Must Be a Party	Court Approval	Legal Enforceability	Termination/ Modification
	agreements are unenforceable.	tion agency if one was involved.	test. See VT. STAT. ANN. tit. 15A, §§ 4–112 (b)(1)–(6)	ent adoption may be enforced by a civil action only if the court finds it in the best interests of the child. Failure to comply is not grounds for setting aside the adoption.	modification; or (b) exceptional circumstances have arisen to justify the modification.
Virginia VA. CODE ANN. § 63.2– 1220.2 to 1220.4 (2012).	May include any types of contact. Agreements must contain provisions regarding the adoption being irrevocable, and birth parent(s) rights of enforcement. *See* VA. CODE ANN. § 63.2– 1220.2	The birth parent(s), the adoptive parent(s).	Court will approve agreement if it finds that it is in the best interests of the child, the adoptive and birth parent(s) consent, a child age 14 or over consents, and several other requirements for	To be enforceable the agreement shall be approved by the court and incorporated into the final decree of adoption. Failure to comply is not grounds for setting aside the adoption. Can't award	Court may modify agreement at any time, after notice and opportunity to be heard of both parties, the court determines it is in the child's best interest to modify the agreement. To modify, there must be a change in circumstances that has affected the best in-

State & Statute	What May/ Must Be Included in Post adoption Contract Agreements	Who May/ Must Be a Party	Court Approval	Legal Enforceability	Termination/ Modification
	(B)		adoptions through an agency. VA. CODE ANN. § 63.2–1220.3	monetary damages.	terests of the child.
Washington WASH. REV. CODE § 26.33.295 (2012).	Agreements may permit communication or contact between adopted children, adoptive parent(s), and birth parent(s).	Adoptive and biological parent(s).	The court may approve an agreement if it finds it is in the best interests of the child.	An agreement may be enforced by a civil action and the prevailing party may be awarded attorney's fees. Failure to comply is not grounds for setting aside the adoption.	An agreement may not be modified unless the court finds it is in the best interests of the child and: (a) the persons subject to the order request the modification; or (b) exceptional circumstances have arisen to justify the modification.
West Virginia W. VA. CODE § 48–22–704 (2012).	Not addressed statutorily.	Not addressed statutorily.	Not addressed statutorily.	The court may hear a petition to enforce the agreement and do so if it finds it is in the best interests of the child. Failure to comply is	Not addressed statutorily.

State & Statute	What May/ Must Be Included in Post adoption Contract Agreements	Who May/ Must Be a Party	Court Approval	Legal Enforceability	Termination/ Modification
				not grounds for setting aside the adoption.	
Wisconsin Wis. Stat. § 48.925 (2011).	May grant reasonable visitation rights.	Adoptive parent(s), birth parent(s), or any person who has maintained a parent-like relationship with the child.	Court determines if visitation is in best interest of the child, and the party seeking visitation will not undermine or affect the parenting decisions of the adoptive parent(s). Whenever possible, the court shall consider the wishes of the child.	Any person who interferes with visitation may be proceeded against for contempt of court.	Not statutorily addressed.

Omitted states: The following states have no statutory provisions for post-adoption contact: Alabama, Arkansas, Colorado, Delaware, Georgia, Hawaii, Idaho, Illinois, Iowa, Kansas, Kentucky, Maine, Michigan, Mississippi, New Jersey, North Dakota, Pennsylvania, Utah, or Wyoming.

IV. Access to Adoption Records

Historically, the secrecy that surrounded adoption was based on the idea that adoption was designed to fully integrate the adopted child into his adoptive family. As stated earlier, in the past, adoption was meant to imitate nature, which formed the basis for placement standards. The process was so secret that some states allowed original birth certificates to be altered, resulting in the original entry to be changed and the names of the adoptive parents to be substituted for the birth parents. In those instances, adopted children would find it almost impossible to locate their birth parents if their only source was the birth record. Today, upon the finalization of adoption, the original birth certificate is sealed and held by the state's register of vital records and a new birth certificate is issued to the adopted child. The new birth certificate lists the adoptive parents as the parents of record.

There is no uniformity among the jurisdictions with regard to access to either court records or original birth certificates. In order to have access to the original birth certificate, the majority of jurisdictions require a court order. At least two states, Idaho and Mississippi, require the consent of all parties in order for the original birth certificates to be available to an adopted person. Alabama (age nineteen) and Alaska (age eighteen) allow adult adopted persons to obtain their records. Mostly, court adoption records are sealed and not available for inspection by the parties involved or the public.

During the 1970s, efforts were made by adopted children, now adults, to search for their birth parents. In the limited number of American jurisdictions which allowed access to court adoption records, the judge would have to be convinced that the reason for access was for "good cause." Ordinarily, that was defined as meaning for medical reasons.

Today, access to adoption records is less formidable. A distinction is made between identifying information and non-identifying information. Non-identifying information, to which all states now allow access, includes date and place of the adopted person's birth, age and physical description of her birth parents, their race, ethnicity, religion and education, as well as their occupation and medical history.

Identifying information refers to information that would lead to the positive identification of either an adopted person or her birth parents. Examples would include actual name, address and contact information. Some states have a mutual consent registry, which serves as a clearing house for obtaining information. The procedure for obtaining information from the registry varies from state to state, but most require consent of at least one parent and an adopted person over the age of majority. If the birth parent has not consented to having her child learn the birth parent's identity and there is a medical necessity, for example, it is possible for a judge to issue a court order releasing the information. In some states, the siblings of the adopted child may also obtain information about the adopted child.

In addition to the legal aspects to an adopted child, now an adult, obtaining information about his or her birth parents there are psychological issues. In 1973, Dr. John Triseliotis' book, "In Search of Origins" was published in Great Britain by Rutledge & Kegan Paul, Ltd., and in 1975 the American edition was published by Beacon Press. The author, a psychiatric social worker, was the first to undertake a major psychological research project involving adopted adults' applying for information about their birth parents in Scotland. He was interested in examining the motivation for the adopted person's search, and the use to which they would put the information. The results of the research are valuable for social workers and attorneys in counseling those who seek the information and for judges in deciding whether to release the information. Even though the research was undertaken in Scotland over thirty years ago, it was based on solid psychological theory that transcends geography. One learned from the research that simple curiosity was not the explanation for the search, but that it involved much deeper psychological reasons having a great deal to do with issues of separation and loss facing the adopted person. For example, the death of an adoptive parent may be the catalyst for searching for the adult adopted child's birth parents, or the adopted child's leaving his adoptive parents' house and beginning college may invoke feelings of separation. Both those events may explain the timing of the search and provide the focus for the counseling. In addition, adopted children may be searching in order to learn more about themselves including their ethnic background and personal characteristics.

A.   Access to Identifying Information

State	Statutory Citation	What Nonidentifying Information/Is it Available to Birth Parents and/or Siblings	Access to Identifying Information	Access to Original Birth Certificate
		**All states, in their adoption statutes, have a provision allowing an adoptive parent of a minor access to non-identifying information about the minor's birth family.		
Alabama	ALA. CODE. §§ 22–9A–12(c)–(d), 26–10A–31 (2012).	Nonidentifying information includes health and medical history of birth parents and the adopted person, general family background, physical descriptions, the length of time the child was in out-of-home care other than with the adoptive parents, and the circumstances resulting in the adoption. Birth parents may access nonidentifying information about the child.	Utilize a mutual consent system, but when the consent is not on record a confidential intermediary may be used.	Available to the adopted person upon written request at age 19.
Alaska	ALASKA STAT.	Nonidentifying information includes	The current name and	An uncertified copy is

State	Statutory Citation	What Nonidentifying Information/Is it Available to Birth Parents and/or Siblings	Access to Identifying Information	Access to Original Birth Certificate
	§§ 18.50. 500, 510 (2012).	the age of the birth parents at the child's birth, the birth parents' heritage, including ethnic background and tribal membership, the medical history of the birth parents and blood relatives of the birth parents, the number of years of school completed by the birth parents when the child was born, the physical description of the birth parents, the existence of other children of the birth parents, the religion of the birth parents, whether the birth parents were alive at the time of the adoption and other information provided by the birth parents including photos and letters.	address of the adopted child may be disclosed to the birth parent upon request if the child is eighteen or older and has requested in writing that the information be disclosed upon request of the birth parent.	available to the adopted person upon written request at age 18.
Arizona	ARIZ. REV. STAT. ANN. §§ 8–121, 129; 36–337 (2012).	Nonidentifying information includes health and genetic history of the birth parents and members of the birth parents' families. Birth parents and adult birth siblings may access nonidentifying information about the child.	Available upon mutual agreement shown to the court or upon motion to the court.	Available upon court order or as prescribed by rule.
Arkansas	ARK. CODE ANN. §§ 9–	Nonidentifying information includes	Mutual consent regis-	Available upon court

State	Statutory Citation	What Nonidentifying Information/Is it Available to Birth Parents and/or Siblings	Access to Identifying Information	Access to Original Birth Certificate
	9–504, 505; 20–18–406 (2011).	the health, genetic, and social history of the child. Birth parents may access nonidentifying information about the child.	try is used.	order or as provided by regulation.
California	CAL. FAM. CODE §§ 8706, 8817, 9201–9206 (2012); CAL. HEALTH & SAFETY CODE § 102705 (2012).	Nonidentifying information includes medical history, scholastic information, psychological evaluations, and developmental history. Access is restricted to adopting parents only.	Identifying information for birth parents, birth siblings and adopted persons aged twenty-one or older may be disclosed upon request if the affected party has consented in writing or it is deemed necessary because of a medical emergency. If an adult adopted person and the birth parents have each consented contact may be arranged.	Available upon court order.
Colorado	COL. REV. STAT. §§ 19–5–304, 305 (2012).	Nonidentifying information includes the physical description of the birth parents, the educational background of the birth parents, genetic in-	Mutual consent registry is used with birth parents listing a contact preference	Available when consent to the release of identifying information from the birth par-

State	Statutory Citation	What Nonidentifying Information/Is it Available to Birth Parents and/or Siblings	Access to Identifying Information	Access to Original Birth Certificate
		formation about the birth family, medical information about the adopted person's birth, social information about the birth parents and placement history of the adopted person. Birth parents and adult birth siblings may access nonidentifying information about the child.	regarding contact by an adult adopted person, though a confidential intermediary may be used upon motion to the court.	ents are on file.
Connecticut	CONN. GEN. STAT. §§ 45A– 746, 753 (2012).	Nonidentifying information about the birth parents includes their age at the time of the child's birth, their ethnic background and nationality, their general physical appearance, the time of the child's birth, their education, occupation, talents, hobbies, and special interests, the existence of any other children born to either parent, health history of they and their relatives, their reasons for placing the child for adoption, their religion and any other relevant information. Birth parents may access nonidentifying information about the child.	Any authorized applicant may request that the child-placing agency or department release identifying information. This information should be released unless the consent of the person whose information is to be released has not been given or the release would be seriously disruptive to or endanger the physical or emotional health of	Available upon court order.

State	Statutory Citation	What Nonidentifying Information/Is it Available to Birth Parents and/or Siblings	Access to Identifying Information	Access to Original Birth Certificate
			the applicant or the person whose identity is being requested.	
Delaware	DEL. CODE ANN. tit. 13, §§ 923, 924, 929, 962 (2011).	Statute does not specify what nonidentifying information is available. Birth parents may access nonidentifying information about the child.	Mutual consent registry is used.	The adopted person over twenty-one may request a copy unless the birth parent has filed an affidavit denying release of identifying information.
District of Columbia	D.C. CODE §§ 16–311, 314 (2012).	Not addressed statutorily.	Available upon court order finding that the welfare of the child is promoted.	Available upon court order.
Florida	FLA. STAT. § 63.162 (2012).	Nonidentifying information includes family medical history and social history of the adopted person and the birth parents.	Mutual consent registry is used.	Available upon court order.
Georgia	GA. CODE ANN. §§ 19–8–23; 31–10–14 (2011).	Nonidentifying information includes date and place of the adopted person's birth and genetic, social, and health history of the birth parents.	Mutual consent registry is used.	Available upon court order or as provided by statute.
Hawaii	HAWAII REV. STAT. §§ 338–20; 578–14, 14.5, 15 (2011).	Nonidentifying information includes medical information on the birth parents regarding the adopted child's	Mutual consent registry is used, but information will be released	Available upon court order.

State	Statutory Citation	What Nonidentifying Information/Is it Available to Birth Parents and/or Siblings	Access to Identifying Information	Access to Original Birth Certificate
		potential genetic or other inheritable diseases.	unless the affected party has filed a non-consent.	
Idaho	IDAHO CODE ANN. §§ 16–1506; 39–258, 259A (2012).	Nonidentifying information includes a copy of all medical and genetic information compiled as part of the adoption investigation. Access is restricted to adopting parents only.	Mutual consent registry is used.	Available upon court order or when all parties have consented.
Illinois	410 ILL. COMP. STAT. 535/17 (2011), 750 ILL. COMP. STAT. 50/18.05, 18.1, 18.3(a), 18.4 (2011).	Nonidentifying information includes the birth parent's age, race, religion, ethnic background, general physical appearance, education, occupation, hobbies, interests, talents, and other children. It also includes information about birth grandparents, their reason for emigrating into the United States, if applicable, and country of origin, the relationship between the birth parents, detailed medical and mental histories of the child, birth parents and immediate relatives and the actual date and place of the birth of the adopted person.	Mutual consent registry is used, though a confidential intermediary may be used to obtain medical information.	For adoptions finalized prior to 2000, available upon court order or as provided by regulation. For adoptions finalized since 2000, available to persons who have established their eligibility by registering with state adoption agency.
Indiana	IND. CODE §§ 31–19–13–2; 31–	Nonidentifying information includes all available social,	Mutual consent registry is used,	For adoptions finalized after

State	Statutory Citation	What Nonidentifying Information/Is it Available to Birth Parents and/or Siblings	Access to Identifying Information	Access to Original Birth Certificate
	19–17–3, 5; 31–19–22–2; 31–19–25–2, 3, 6, 8, 9 (2011).	medical, psychological and educational records concerning the child.	but information will be released unless the affected party has filed a non-consent for adoptions finalized after 1993.	1993, available to persons who have established their eligibility by registering with state adoption agency.
Iowa	IOWA CODE §§ 144.24, 144.43A, 600.16 (2012).	Nonidentifying information includes medical history, medical and developmental histories, and social history of the person to be adopted.	Mutual consent registry is used.	Available upon court order.
Kansas	KAN. STAT. ANN. §§ 59–2122, 65–2423 (2011).	Nonidentifying information is not defined, but may be exchanged in the event of a health or medical need.	Identifying information shall not be shared with the birth parents without the permission of the adoptive parents of the minor child or the adopted adult.	Available upon court order or demand of the adult adopted person.
Kentucky	KY. REV. STAT. ANN. §§ 199. 520, 570, 572, 575 (2011).	Nonidentifying information includes the health history and other nonidentifying background information of the birth parents and blood relatives of the adopted person.	Adoptive parents may be given access if there is a consent on record from the birth parents, a consent is later obtained by an intermediary or access is or-	Available upon court order.

186 THE ADOPTIVE RELATIONSHIP Pt. 2

State	Statutory Citation	What Nonidentifying Information/Is it Available to Birth Parents and/or Siblings	Access to Identifying Information	Access to Original Birth Certificate
			dered by the court. If mutual consent exists among birth siblings they may be given contact information as well.	
Louisiana	LA. CHILD. CODE. arts. 1125, 27, 27.1, 1270 (2011); LA. REV. STAT. § 40:73 (2011).	Nonidentifying information includes a statement of family history, containing nonidentifying medical and genetic information. Birth parents may access nonidentifying information about the child.	Mutual consent registry is used.	Available upon court order only upon showing of a compelling reason why such disclosure is necessary
Maine	ME. REV. STAT. tit. 18–A, § 9–310; tit. 22, §§ 2706–A, 2765, 2766, 8205 (2011).	Nonidentifying information includes a current medical, psychological, and developmental history of the child, including an account of the child's prenatal care, medical condition at birth, results of newborn screening, any drug or medication taken by the child's birth mother, any subsequent medical, psychological, or psychiatric examination, any physical, sexual or emotional abuse suffered by the child, a record of any immunizations and health care re-	Mutual consent registry is used.	Available upon court order or pursuant to 22 MRS § 2768, which allows access to the adopted person upon application to the state registrar when they have reached eighteen years of age.

State	Statutory Citation	What Nonidentifying Information/Is it Available to Birth Parents and/or Siblings	Access to Identifying Information	Access to Original Birth Certificate
		ceived since birth, and relevant information concerning the medical, psychological, and social history of the birth parents.		
Maryland	MD. CODE ANN., FAM. LAW §§ 5–356, 357, 358; 5–3A–42, 5–3B–29, 5–4C–06, 07 (2012).	Nonidentifying information includes a comprehensive medical and mental health history of the prospective adoptive child and pertinent medical and mental health histories of each of the child's birth parents. Birth parents may access nonidentifying information about the child.	Mutual consent registry is used, but information will be released unless the affected party has filed a non-consent for adoptions finalized after 1999.	Available upon request of an adopted person who is at least twenty-one years old unless the birth parent has filed a disclosure veto. Additionally, if adoptee, relative, or former parent urgently needs medical information, the court may appoint an intermediary to contact the adoptee or former parent for the information.
Massachu-setts	MASS. GEN. LAWS ch. 210, §§ 5C, 5D (2012).	Nonidentifying information includes information about the adoptive person and his or her birth parents that does not identify the birth parents or their present or former locations.	Available upon consent of the affected party, but in the case of the adopted person consent must be giv-	Available upon court order.

State	Statutory Citation	What Nonidentifying Information/Is it Available to Birth Parents and/or Siblings	Access to Identifying Information	Access to Original Birth Certificate
		Birth parents may access nonidentifying information about the child.	en by the adoptive parents before the child reaches twenty-one years of age.	
Michigan	MICH. COMP. LAWS §§ 710.27, .68, 333.2882 (2012).	Nonidentifying information includes the date and place of the child's birth, health and genetic history of the child, subsequent medical history of the child while the court had jurisdiction, any neglect or abuse suffered by the child, immunizations and health care record of the child while in foster care, medical/psychological evaluations of the birth parents done at the time of placement, the date and cause of death of a deceased parent, a description of the child's family origin, child's past relationship with any birth relative, levels of education, achievement of the child's family, hobbies and special interests of the child's family, circumstances of any order terminating parental rights of a parent, length of time between such a termination and	Mutual consent registry is used, but information will be released unless the affected party has filed a nonconsent for adoptions finalized before May 28, 1948 or after September 12, 1980. Confidential intermediary may also be used to locate an adult adopted person.	Available upon court order or upon written request of the adult adopted person when accompanied by a central adoption registry clearance form.

State	Statutory Citation	What Nonidentifying Information/Is it Available to Birth Parents and/or Siblings	Access to Identifying Information	Access to Original Birth Certificate
		adoption and any information necessary to determine the child's eligibility for state or federal benefits. Birth parents and adult birth siblings may access nonidentifying information about the child.		
Minnesota	MINN. STAT. §§ 259.83, 89 (2012).	Nonidentifying information includes the detailed medical and social history that was provided at the time of adoption and current nonidentifying social and medical history of the adopted person's birth family.	Information will be released upon request unless the affected party has filed a nonconsent for adoptions finalized after July of 1982.	For adoptions finalized prior to August of 1977, the adopted person may petition the court for disclosure and the petition should be granted if the court determines that disclosure would be of greater benefit than non-disclosure. For adoptions finalized after August of 1977, available upon request of the adopted person if there is no affidavit for nondisclosure on file for an adopted per-

State	Statutory Citation	What Nonidentifying Information/Is it Available to Birth Parents and/or Sib-lings	Access to Identifying Information	Access to Original Birth Certificate
				son over 19 years of age. Before re-leasing the information, the Com-missioner of Human Ser-vices' agent or a licensed child-plac-ing agency must make reasonable efforts to notify each parent of the right, within 30 days, to file an affidavit of non-dis-closure.
Mississippi	MISS. CODE ANN. §§ 93–17– 205, 207, 209, 215, 217, 219, 221 (2011).	Nonidentifying in-formation includes medical and social history of the birth parents, a report of any medical exami-nation that either birth parent had within one year be-fore the date of the petition for adop-tion, if available, a report describing the adopted per-son's prenatal care and medical condi-tion at birth, if available, and the medical and social history of the adopted person, in-cluding information regarding genetical-ly-inheritable dis-eases or illnesses,	An adopted person aged twenty-one or older may request information regarding birth par-ents unless that birth parent has executed an affidavit prohibiting the release of such in-formation.	Available upon court order or when all parties have consented.

State	Statutory Citation	What Nonidentifying Information/Is it Available to Birth Parents and/or Siblings	Access to Identifying Information	Access to Original Birth Certificate
		and any other relevant medical, social and genetic information. Birth parents and adult birth siblings may access nonidentifying information about the child.		
Missouri	Mo. Rev. Stat. §§ 193. 125; 453.121 (2011).	Nonidentifying information includes the physical description, nationality, religious background, and medical history of the birth parents or siblings.	Mutual consent registry is used.	Available upon court order.
Montana	Mont. Code Ann. §§ 42–6– 102–104, 109 (2011).	Nonidentifying information is not defined in the statute. Birth parents and adult birth siblings may access nonidentifying information about the child.	Confidential intermediaries are used to determine if there is mutual consent to the exchange of identifying information.	For persons adopted before July 1, 1997, available upon written request of the adopted person. For persons adopted between July 1, 1967 and September 30, 1997, available only upon court order. For person adopted on or after October 1, 1997, available upon written request of an adopted person age eighteen or

State	Statutory Citation	What Nonidentifying Information/Is it Available to Birth Parents and/or Siblings	Access to Identifying Information	Access to Original Birth Certificate
				older unless birth parent requests nondisclosure. The department may still release the birth certificate if required to assist the adopted person to become enrolled in or a member of an Indian tribe.
Nebraska	NEB. REV. STAT. §§ 43–121, 128, 130, 136, 143, 146.02, 146.04 146.05 (2011).	Nonidentifying information includes the available medical history of the adopted person and the birth parents.	Information will be released upon request unless the affected party has filed a nonconsent for adoptions finalized after August of 1998.	Available when consented to the release of identifying information from the birth parents are on file (for adoptions finalized after August 1998).
Nevada	NEV. REV. STAT. §§ 127. 007, 152; 440.310 (2011).	Nonidentifying information includes a copy of any medical records of the child that are in possession of the agency, any information about the medical and sociological history of the child and the birth parents and any behavioral, emotional, or psy-	Mutual consent registry is used.	Available upon court order.

State	Statutory Citation	What Nonidentifying Information/Is it Available to Birth Parents and/or Siblings	Access to Identifying Information	Access to Original Birth Certificate
		chological problems the child may have, and information regarding any subsidies, assistance, and other services that may be available to the child if it is determined that he or she has special needs. Access is restricted to adopting parents only.		
New Hampshire	N.H. REV. STAT. ANN. §§ 170 –B:23, B:24 (2011).	Nonidentifying information includes any nonidentifying social or medical information about the adopted person, the birth parents, or the blood relatives. Birth parents may access nonidentifying information about the child.	A mutual consent system is used, though information may be available upon court order as well.	Available upon court order.
New Jersey	N.J. STAT. ANN. §§ 9:3– 41.1, 52; 26:8–40.1 (2011).	Nonidentifying information includes the child's developmental and medical history, his or her personality and temperament, the birth parent's complete medical histories, any drugs or medications taken during pregnancy, and any other conditions of the birth parent's health that may be a factor in influencing the child's present or future health. Access is restricted	Available only upon court order.	Available upon court order.

State	Statutory Citation	What Nonidentifying Information/Is it Available to Birth Parents and/or Siblings	Access to Identifying Information	Access to Original Birth Certificate
		to adopting parents only.		
New Mexico	N.M. Stat. §§ 24–14–17; 32A–5–40, 41 (2011).	Nonidentifying information includes the health and medical histories of the birth parents and the adopted person, his or her general family background, physical descriptions, and the length of time the adopted person was in the care and custody of persons other than the adoptive parents. Birth parents and adult birth siblings may access nonidentifying information about the child.	A mutual consent system is used, though information may be available upon court order as well.	Available upon court order.
New York	N.Y. Pub. Health Law §§ 4138–c, d (2011).	Nonidentifying information includes the age of the birth parents at birth, the heritage of the parents, their education at the time of the child's birth, their general physical appearance, their religion, their occupation, health history, talents, hobbies, and special interests, the facts and circumstances relating to the adoption, and the existence of any known birth siblings. Birth parents and adult birth siblings may access	Mutual consent registry is used.	Available upon court order.

State	Statutory Citation	What Nonidentifying Information/Is it Available to Birth Parents and/or Siblings	Access to Identifying Information	Access to Original Birth Certificate
		nonidentifying information about the child.		
North Carolina	N.C. GEN. STAT. §§ 48–3–205; 48–9–103, 106, 109 (2011).	Nonidentifying information includes the date of the child's birth, the age of the birth parents at birth, the heritage of the birth parents, their education at the time of birth, their general physical appearance, and all reasonably available nonidentifying information about the health and genetic history of the child, the birth parents, and other members of the birth parents' families. Adult birth siblings may access nonidentifying information about the child	A mutual consent system is used.	Available upon court order.
North Dakota	N.D. CENT. CODE §§ 14–15–01(12), 16, 23–02.1–18 (2011).	The age of the birth parent at birth, their heritage, their education at the time of birth, their general physical appearance, their talents, hobbies, and special interests, the existence of other children they have, the reasons they placed the child for adoption, their vocations, and their health histories and the health	A mutual consent system is used, though consent may be sought if not on file. Adult adopted persons may initiate the process with respect to birth siblings.	Available upon court order or as provided by rules and regulations.

State	Statutory Citation	What Nonidentifying Information/Is it Available to Birth Parents and/or Siblings	Access to Identifying Information	Access to Original Birth Certificate
		histories of their relatives. Birth parents may access nonidentifying information about the child.		
Ohio	OHIO REV. CODE ANN. §§ 3107. 47, 49, 66; 3705.12 (2011).	Nonidentifying information is not defined by the statute. Birth parents and adult birth siblings may access nonidentifying information about the child.	Mutual consent registry is used, but information will be released unless the affected party has filed a non-consent.	Available upon court order or upon request of the adopted person or adoptive parent unless a nondisclosure affidavit is on file.
Oklahoma	OKLA. STAT. tit. 10, §§ 7505– 6.6; 7508–1.2, 1.3 (2011).	Nonidentifying information includes medical or social history either volunteered by the person whose information is requested or obtained by a confidential intermediary. Birth parents and adult birth siblings may access nonidentifying information about the child.	Mutual consent registry is used, though administered through the use of confidential intermediaries.	For adoptions after November 1, 1997, available upon court order, or upon written request of an adopted person eighteen years or older provided the birth parents have not filed affidavits of nondisclosure and there are no birth siblings under age eighteen in an adoptive family whose

State	Statutory Citation	What Nonidentifying Information/Is it Available to Birth Parents and/or Siblings	Access to Identifying Information	Access to Original Birth Certificate
				whereabouts are known.
Oregon	Or. Rev. Stat. Ann. § 109.455, .460, 500; 432.230 (2012).	Nonidentifying information includes a genetic and social history and health history that excludes identifying information, if available. Birth parents may access nonidentifying information about the child.	Mutual consent registry is used.	Available upon court order or as provided by rule of the state registrar.
Pennsylvania	23 Pa. Cons. Stat. §§ 2921–25 (2011).	Nonidentifying information includes the home study and placement report and as much information concerning the adopted person's birth parents as will not endanger the anonymity of the birth parents. Birth parents may access nonidentifying information about the child.	Mutual consent registry is used.	Available when consent to the release of identifying information from the birth parents are on file.
Rhode Island	R.I. Gen. Laws §§ 15-7. 2–1, 2, 7, 9, 12 (2011).	Nonidentifying information includes medical history, health status, cause of and age of death, height, weight, eye and hair color, ethnic origins, religion and health history of the adult adopted person, birth parents and other specified persons. Birth parents and adult birth siblings may access	Mutual consent registry is used.	An uncertified copy is available to the adopted person when each birth parent named on the certificate has registered with the adoption registry.

State	Statutory Citation	What Nonidentifying Information/Is it Available to Birth Parents and/or Siblings	Access to Identifying Information	Access to Original Birth Certificate
		nonidentifying information about the child.		
South Carolina	S.C. CODE ANN. §§ , 44–63–140 (2011).	Nonidentifying information includes the health and medical histories of the birth parents and adopted person, the adopted person's general family background without name references or geographical designations, and the length of time the adopted person has been in the care and custody of the adoptive parent. Birth parents and adult birth siblings may access nonidentifying information about the child.	Mutual consent registry is used.	Access not specified by statute.
South Dakota	S.D. CODIFIED LAWS §§ 25–6–15.2, 15.3; 34–25–16.1, 16.4 (2011).	Nonidentifying information includes the age of the birth parents at birth, the heritage of the parents, their education at the time of the child's birth, their general physical appearance, their talents, hobbies, and special interests, the existence of other children born to either parent before the child's birth, whether termination was voluntary or involun-	Mutual consent registry is used.	Available upon court order.

State	Statutory Citation	What Nonidentifying Information/Is it Available to Birth Parents and/or Siblings	Access to Identifying Information	Access to Original Birth Certificate
		tary, the religion of the birth parents, their occupation in general terms, their and their blood relatives' health history, and the relationship between the birth parents.		
Tennessee	TENN. CODE ANN. §§ 36–1–128, 129, 130, 133 (2012).	Nonidentifying information includes the date and time of the child's birth, the child's weight and other physical characteristics at birth, the age of the adopted person's blood relatives at birth, the nationality, ethnic background, race and religious preference of the birth or legal relatives, the educational level, general occupation, and talents and hobbies of birth or legal relatives, a general physical description of birth or legal relatives, whether the birth or legal parent had any other children and the health history of the adopted person and blood or legal relatives including psychological or psychiatric information. Birth parents may access nonidentifying in-	Mutual consent registry is used.	Available to persons who have established their eligibility by registering with a state adoption agency.

State	Statutory Citation	What Nonidentifying Information/Is it Available to Birth Parents and/or Siblings	Access to Identifying Information	Access to Original Birth Certificate
		formation about the child.		
Texas	TEX. FAM. CODE ANN. §§ 162. 018, 407, 413, 414, 416 (2011). TEX. HEALTH & SAFETY CODE § 192.008 (2011).	Nonidentifying information includes copies of records that have been edited to protect the identity of the birth parents and other information relating to the history of the adopted person.	Mutual consent registry is used.	Available upon court order.
Utah	UTAH CODE ANN. §§ 78B–6– 141, 143, 144 (2011).	Nonidentifying information includes a detailed health history and a genetic and social history of the adopted person. Birth parents and adult birth siblings may access nonidentifying information about the child.	Mutual consent registry is used.	Available upon court order.
Vermont	VT. STAT. ANN. tit. 15A, §§ 6–104 TO 107 (2012).	Nonidentifying information includes a social and health history of the child, any abuse known to have been suffered by the child, his or her enrollment and performance in school including results of testing and any special educational needs, an account of the child's past relationships with any relative, foster parent, or other person and a social and	Mutual consent registry is used, but information will be released unless the affected party has filed a non-consent for adoptions finalized after June of 1986.	Available to persons who have established their eligibility by registering with a state adoption agency. Also, becomes unsealed ninety-nine years after the adopted person's birth.

State	Statutory Citation	What Nonidentifying Information/Is it Available to Birth Parents and/or Siblings	Access to Identifying Information	Access to Original Birth Certificate
		health history of the minor's extended family including: health and genetic history, racial, ethnic and religious background, general physical description, education, vocational, athletic, artistic, or scientific achievement or interests and the existence of any other child of the parents. Birth parents and adult birth siblings may access nonidentifying information about the child.		
Virginia	VA. CODE ANN. §§ 32.1–261; 63.2–1246, 1247 (2011).	Nonidentifying information is not defined in the statute.	A system of mutual consent is used, though consent is only one factor in the Commissioner's decision of whether or not to release the information.	Available upon court order.
Washington	WASH. REV. CODE ANN. §§ 26.33.340, 343–347, 380 (2012).	Nonidentifying information includes a report including a chronological history of the circumstances surrounding the adoptive placement any available psychiatric reports, psychological reports, court reports pertaining to depen-	A system of mutual consent is used, though administered through confidential intermediaries.	Available to the birth parent upon request and for adoptions finalized after September 1993, available upon request of the adopted person age

State	Statutory Citation	What Nonidentifying Information/Is it Available to Birth Parents and/or Siblings	Access to Identifying Information	Access to Original Birth Certificate
		dency or custody or school reports. Birth parents may access nonidentifying information about the child.		eighteen or older provided the birth parent has not filed an affidavit of nondisclosure.
West Virginia	W. Va. Code Ann. §§ 16–5–18; 48–23–501 to 504, 601 (2012).	Nonidentifying information includes a detailed written health history and genetic and social history of the child. Birth parents may access nonidentifying information about the child.	Mutual consent registry is used.	Available upon court order.
Wisconsin	Wis. Stat. §§ 48.432, 433 (2011).	Nonidentifying information includes information voluntarily given by a birth parent or given upon order by the court as well as any information the agency or department receives from a physician stating that a birth parent has acquired or may have a genetically transferable disease.	A system of mutual consent is used, though consent may be sought if not on file. The information may also be released upon court order.	Available when consent to the release of identifying information from the birth parents are on file.
Wyoming	Wy. Stat. Ann. §§ 1–22–116, 203; 35–1–417 (2011).	Nonidentifying information includes the medical history of the adoptive child and his or her birth parents including conditions or diseases believed to be hereditary, any drugs or medication taken during pregnancy by the mother, and any	A confidential intermediary system is used.	Available upon court order.

State	Statutory Citation	What Nonidentifying Information/Is it Available to Birth Parents and/or Siblings	Access to Identifying Information	Access to Original Birth Certificate
		other information that may be a factor influencing the child's present or future health.		

B. Access to Non–Identifying Information[3]

State	Citation	Access by Adult Adoptee	Access by Birth Parents	Access by Birth Siblings	Special Procedures[4]	Requests for Additional Information[5]
Alabama	ALA. CODE § 26–10A–31 (2012).	P	P	NP		Available
Alaska	ALASKA STAT. § 18.50.510 (2012).	P	NA	NP		
Arizona	ARIZ. REV. STAT. ANN. §§ 8–121, 129 (2012).	P	P	NP		
Arkansas	ARK. CODE ANN. § 9–9–505 (2011).	P	P	NP		
California	CAL. FAM. CODE §§ 8706, 8817 (2012).	Through adoptive parents only	NA	NA		
Colorado	COLO. REV. STAT. § 19–5–	P	P	NA		

3.   All states allow adoptive parents access to non-identifying information. This chart addresses issues regarding which states differ.

State	Citation	Access by Adult Adoptee	Access by Birth Parents	Access by Birth Siblings	Special Procedures[4]	Requests for Additional Information[5]
	305 (2012).					
Connecticut	CONN. GEN. STAT. § 45A–746 (2012).	P	P	NP		
Delaware	DEL. CODE ANN. tit. 13 § 924 (2011).	P	P	NP		
Florida	FLA. STAT. § 63.162 (2012).	P	NA	NP		
Georgia	GA. CODE ANN. § 19–8–23 (2011).	P	Parties at interest	NP		
Hawaii	HAW. REV. STAT. §§ 578–14.5, 15 (2011).	P	Parties at interest	NP		
Idaho	IDAHO CODE ANN. § 16–1506 (2012).	Through adoptive parents only	NA	NA		
Illinois	750 ILL. COMP. STAT. 50/18.4 (2011).	P	NA	NA		Available
Indiana	IND. CODE §§ 31–19–17–3, 5 (2011).	P	NA	NA		
Iowa	IOWA CODE § 600.16 (2012).	P	NP	NP		
Kansas	KAN. STAT. ANN. § 59–	P	Not permitted after the	NP		Available

State	Citation	Access by Adult Adoptee	Access by Birth Parents	Access by Birth Siblings	Special Procedures[4]	Requests for Additional Information[5]
	2122 (2011).		decree of adoption is entered			
Kentucky	KY. REV. STAT. ANN. § 199. 520 (2011).	P	NA	NA		
Louisiana	LA. CHILD. CODE ANN. arts. 1126, 1127 (2011).	P	P	NA		
Maine	ME. REV. STAT. ANN. tit. 18–A, § 9–310; 22, § 8205 (2011).	P	NP	NP		Available
Maryland	MD. CODE. ANN., FAM. LAW § 5–356 to 358 (2012).	P	NA	NA		Available
Massachusetts	MASS. GEN. LAWS ch. 210, § 5D (2011).	P	P	NA		Available
Michigan	MICH. COMP. LAWS §§ 710.27, 68 (2012).	P	P	P		
Minnesota	MINN. STAT. § 259.83 (2012).	P	NA	NA		Available
Mississippi	MISS. CODE ANN.	P	P	P		Available

State	Citation	Access by Adult Adoptee	Access by Birth Parents	Access by Birth Siblings	Special Procedures[4]	Requests for Additional Information[5]
	§ 93–17–205–209 (2011).					
Missouri	Mo. Rev. Stat. § 453.121 (2011).	P	NP	NP		
Montana	Mont. Code Ann. § 42–6–102 (2011).	P	P	P		
Nebraska	Neb. Rev. Stat. §§ 43–128, 146.02 (2011).	P	NA	NA		
Nevada	Nev. Rev. Stat. § 127.152 (2011).	NA	NA	NA		
New Hampshire	N.H. Rev. Stat. Ann. §§ 170:B–23, 24 (2011).	P	P	NP		
New Jersey	N.J. Stat. Ann. § 9:3–41.1 (2011).	NA	NA	NA		
New Mexico	N.M. Stat. § 32A–5–40 (2011).	P	P	P		
New York	N.Y. Pub. Health Law §§ 4138–C, D (2011).	P	P	P	Must register with State adoption registry to receive information	

State	Citation	Access by Adult Adoptee	Access by Birth Parents	Access by Birth Siblings	Special Procedures[4]	Requests for Additional Information[5]
North Carolina	N.C. Gen. Stat. §§ 48–3–205; 48–9–103 (2011).	P	P	NA		
North Dakota	N.D. Cent. Code §§ 14–15–01(12), (16) (2011).	P	P	NP		
Ohio	Ohio Rev. Code Ann. §§ 3107.60(B); 66 (2011).	P	P	P		
Oklahoma	Okla. Stat. tit. 10 § 7508–1.3 (2011).	P	P	P	Must register with State adoption registry to receive information	
Oregon	Or. Rev. Stat. § 109.500 (2012).	P	P	NP		
Pennsylvania	23 Pa. Cons. Stat. § 2921–25 (2011).	P	NP	P		
Rhode Island	R.I. Gen. Laws §§ 15–7.2–1 to 7.2–7 (2011).	P	P	P	Must register with State adoption registry to receive information	
South Carolina	S.C. Code Ann.	P	P	NP	The release of	

State	Citation	Access by Adult Adoptee	Access by Birth Parents	Access by Birth Siblings	Special Procedures[4]	Requests for Additional Information[5]
	§ 63–9–780 (2011).				information is at the sole discretion of the head of the agency, if she determines it to be in the best interests of the person concerned.	
South Dakota	S.D. CODIFIED LAWS § 25–6–15.2 (2012).	P	NA	NA		
Tennessee	TENN. CODE ANN. § 36–1–133 (2012).	P	P	NP		
Texas	TEX. FAM. CODE ANN. § 162.018 (2011).	P	NA	NA		
Utah	UTAH CODE ANN. § 78B–6–143 (2011).	P	P	P		
Vermont	VT. STAT. ANN. tit. 15A, §§ 2–105; 6–104 (2012).	P	P	P		
Virginia	VA. CODE ANN. § 63.2–	P	NP	NP		

State	Citation	Access by Adult Adoptee	Access by Birth Parents	Access by Birth Siblings	Special Procedures[4]	Requests for Additional Information[5]
	1246 (2011).					
Washington	Wash. Rev. Code §§ 26.33. 340; 380 (2012).	P	P	NP		
West Virginia	W. Va. Code § 48–23–601 (2012).	P	P	NP		
Wisconsin	Wis. Stat. §§ 48. 432, 433 (2011).	P	NP	NP		
Wyoming	Wyo. Stat. Ann. § 1–22–116 (2011).	P	NP	NP		Available

[4]   In general, non-identifying information is obtained by making a written request with the state's adoption registry or similar state agency. Some states, however, require additional steps, which are noted in this column.

[5]   Some states allow the adoptive parents to request that the state adoption registry seek additional non-identifying information from the birth parents where medically necessary. These states are noted in this column.

V.   Equitable Adoption

Not infrequently, the law utilizes legal fictions to achieve equitable results. In marriage, for example, when a man acts as if he is the husband of a woman and later in a court proceeding and when it is to his financial advantage denies that he is, a court in a state that recognizes the doctrine "marriage by estoppel" might apply that doctrine to protect the innocent wife.

Marriage and adoption share in the requirement of the need for documentation. In the case of marriage, there is the requirement of a license and a formal ceremony with witnesses. Twelve American jurisdictions–Alabama, Colorado, District of Columbia, Iowa, Kansas, Montana, Oklahoma, Pennsylvania, Rhode Island, South Carolina, Texas and Utah—however, recognize informal marriage called common law marriage, but even that status has certain requirements like living together with the intent to be married and recognition by the community that the couple are spouses. Once established, common law marriage enjoys the same legal status as a ceremonial marriage.

Common law marriage partners, for example, are subject to the same legal rights and obligations assigned to ceremonial married couples. Children born to a couple living in a common law marriage relationship are legitimate. In order to terminate a common law marriage partners must seek a formal divorce. In a jurisdiction that recognizes common law marriage, if a common law spouse died intestate, his or her spouse inherits in the same way that a formally married spouse would and if the deceased spouse died testate, the common law spouse would take under the will as a surviving spouse.

There is no common law adoption. As stated earlier, adoption is no longer considered a private act, but requires a judicial proceeding. However, there is an exception and this exception shows some similarity to informal marriage in the sense that there is no formal documentation of the adoption but a holding out and an intent on the part of the parents to treat the child as a member of the family.

"De facto adoption," "adoption by estoppel" and "virtual adoption" are terms used in a judicial proceeding involving the estate of a parent. They describe the rights of children in a decedents estates matter or wrongful death action who have assumed the status of an adopted child but lack the formal documentation. Normally, unless a child has been legally adopted, that child does not enjoy the status of a child born to the decedent parent under state inheritance laws. In the judicial proceeding the clear and convincing evidentiary standard is applied to determine whether the child seeking to be an heir was considered the equitably adopted child of the decedent.

In *Wheeling Dollar Savings & Trust Co. v. Singer*, 250 S.E.2d 369 (W. Va. 1978), for example, an eight or nine year old child, Ada, was taken from an orphanage by Lyda Wharton and lived with her, believing she was her adopted daughter since Lyda had held her out in the community as such. Years later after Lyda died, Ada sought her share of Lyda's estate, seeking a declaratory judgment that she was Lyda's heir. A search of the adoption records in Ohio and West Virginia did not reveal that she had been formally adopted, yet the West Virginia Supreme Court was willing to entertain the possibility that Ada was Lyda's adopted child through the application of the doctrine of equitable adoption. In remanding the case for further proceedings, the court provided Ada the opportunity to prove "by clear, cogent and convincing evidence" that Lyda treated her as if she were her formally adopted child, thus allowing her to share in Lyda's estate as a natural child. In the court's opinion, the conditions that had to be met in order to be considered an equitably adopted child included "the benefits of love and affection accruing to the adopting party . . ., the performances of services by the child . . .; the surrender of ties by the natural parent . . .; the society, companionship and filial obedience of the child . . .; and invalid or ineffectual adoption proceeding . . .; reliance by the adopted person upon the existence of his adoptive status . . .; the representation to all the world that the child is a natural or adopted child . . .; and the rearing of the child from an age of tender years by the adopting parents . . ." *Id.* at 374–75. Those conditions reflect the existence of an implied contract of adoption of one kind or another. *Id.* at 375. In another part of the opinion the judge refers to the equitably adopted child as one who should not be subject to discrimination because of what the child has contributed as a member of the family. *Id.* at 374.

A.   Equitable Adoption Statutes

State	Statutory Citations and Relevant cases
Alabama	ALA. CODE 1975 § 26–10A–6 (2012).

State	Statutory Citations and Relevant cases
	"Adoption is purely statutory; it was never recognized by the rules of the common law." *Hanks v. Hanks,* 281 Ala. 92, 99, 199 So.2d 169, 176 (1967). "Equitable adoption is rarely recognized in Alabama and generally requires a finding of an intent to adopt." *J.N.H. v. N.T.H.,* 705 So.2d 448, 452 (Ala.Civ.App.1997), citing *C.H.H. v. R.H.,* 696 So.2d 1076 (Ala.Civ.App. 1996); and see *Hebert v. Stephenson,* 574 So.2d 835 (Ala.Civ.App.1990). "On those rare occasions when this Court or the Court of Civil Appeals has recognized an equitable adoption, it has recognized it only when a definite contract was clearly proven, not only to adopt, but to adopt so as to permit the adoptee to inherit, and the contract was one for which specific performance could be enforced." *C.H.H. v. R.H.,* supra., at 1078, citing *Prince v. Prince,* 194 Ala. 455, 69 So. 906 (1915). *Samek v. Sanders*, 788 So.2d 872, 876 (Ala. 2000).
Alaska	ALASKA STAT. § 13.06.015 (2012). "After examining extensively the doctrine of equitable adoption, we conclude that it is a sound, equitable tool which, when utilized properly, allows courts to avoid unjust and often intolerable results. We further conclude that this court has the power to recognize such a doctrine within the probate context." *Calista Corp. v. Mann*, 564 P.2d 53, 61 (Alaska 1977) (citation omitted).
Arizona	ARIZ. REV. STAT. ANN. § 8–106 (2012). "Doctrine of equitable adoption applies to a situation involving contract to adopt a child fully performed except for statutory formalities and is applied for benefit of the child in determining its right of inheritance upon death of

State	Statutory Citations and Relevant cases
	person contracting to adopt." *In re Prewitt's Estate*, 498 P.2d 470, 471 (Ariz. Ct.App. 1972).
Arkansas	No—Does not recognize Based on a change of position for claims filed on or after 09/28/05 or pending on that date, Arkansas has not recognized equitable adoption since at least 1984.
California	CAL. PROB. CODE § 6455 (West 2012). "Nothing in this chapter affects or limits application of the judicial doctrine of equitable adoption for the benefit of the child or the child's issue." "For several reasons, we conclude the California law of equitable adoption, which has rested on contract principles, does not recognize an estoppel arising merely from the existence of a familial relationship between the decedent and the claimant. The law of intestate succession is intended to carry out 'the intent a decedent without a will is most likely to have had.'" *In re Estate of Ford*, 82 P.3d 747, 753 (Cal. 2004).
Colorado	COLO. REV. STAT. § 15–11–601 (2012). "[T]he doctrine of equitable adoption is limited to claims made by an equitably adopted child against the estate of an adoptive parent and does not extend to allow an equitably adopted child to take through the adoptive parent from the estate of a more remote ancestor." *Matter of Estate of Jenkins*, 904 P.2d 1316, 1320 (Colo. 1995).
Connecticut	CONN. GEN. STAT. ANN. § 12–344 (West 2012). No—Does not recognize "Adoption establishes the legal relationship of parent and child, with all

State	Statutory Citations and Relevant cases
	the consequences of that relationship, between persons not so related by nature, and creates a status unknown to the common law. It is a purely statutory procedure, and a legal adoption results only if the requirements of the statute are fulfilled. Bailey v. Mars, 138 Conn. 593, 597, 87 A.2d 388; Goshkarian's Appeal, 110 Conn. 463, 465, 148 A. 379; Woodward's Appeal, 81 Conn. 152, 165, 70 A. 453; 2 Locke & Kohn, Conn. Probate Practice § 685. Here, it is conceded that the statutory proceedings for a legal adoption were never undertaken. It follows that although the child may have been treated as, and held out to be, an adopted child, she never acquired the status of an adopted child in the eyes of the law." *Lyman v. Sullivan*, 157 A.2d 759, 760–61 (Conn. 1960).
Delaware	"Adoption by estoppel is usually applied to someone who has expressed the intention to adopt, but has not followed through with the statutory formalities. The doctrine finds its most frequent application where a person is permitted to inherit as an adopted child from his foster parents." *Matthews on Behalf of Matthews v. Secretary of Health and Human Services*, 810 F.Supp. 587, 590 (D.Del.1992).
District of Columbia	D.C. CODE § 16–2701 (2012). No—Does not recognize "This Court is of the opinion that it should not use its equity power to disturb the District's statutory scheme." " '[I]t is well established that courts of equity can no more disregard statutory and constitutional provisions than can courts of law.' " *Davis v. Moore,* 772 A.2d 204, 229 (D.C.2001), quoting *Immigration and Naturalization Service v. Pangilinan,* 486 U.S. 875, 883

State	Statutory Citations and Relevant cases
	(1988) (quoting *Hedges v. Dixon County,* 150 U.S. 182, 192 (1893)). "Whether to permit inheritance by one who is neither the natural nor the adopted child of an intestate is a policy issue for the legislative branch." *In re Estate of Lucas,* 2005 WL 674682 (D.C. Super. 2005).Current through July 27, 2011.
Florida	FLA. STAT. ANN. § 731.201 (West 2012). "In the instant case, this Court has found that Beth Angel is the virtually adopted daughter of the decedent. As such, she is entitled to receive the decedent's property under Florida's intestacy statutes." *Williams v. Dorrell*, 714 So. 2d 574, 576 (Fla.Ct.App. 1998).
Georgia	GA. CODE ANN. § 49–4–1 (West 2011). No—Does not recognize "Code Ann. s 99–902, supra, in its definition of 'dependent child' provides among the requirements that such child be one '. . . who is living with his father, mother, grandfather, grandmother, brother, sister, stepfather, stepmother, stepbrother, stepsister, uncle, or aunt, in a place of residence maintained by one or more of such relatives as his or their own home . . .' Compare 42 U.S.C.A. s 606. There is no language in any of the provisions of Code Ann. Ch. 99–9 which could be construed to include a child who had been 'virtually or equitably adopted.' " *Tellis v. Saucier*, 213 S.E.2d 39, 41 (Ga. Ct. App. 1975).
Hawaii	HAW. REV. STAT. § 663–3 (2011). No—Does not recognize "Appellants also urge that we engraft a doctrine of equitable adoption on the law of Hawaii. We explicitly refuse to do so. As pointed out above, we have a

State	Statutory Citations and Relevant cases
	well developed law of adoption in this State and to depart from the statutes by creating a doctrine of equitable adoption would import mischief and uncertainty into the law." *Maui Land & Pineapple Co. v. Makeelani,* 751 P.2d 1020, 1022 (Haw. 1988).
Idaho	No—Does not recognize Idaho Dept. of Health & Welfare v. Doe, 245 P.3d 506 (Idaho App. 2010).
Illinois	750 ILL. COMP. STAT. 50/1 (2011). "In Illinois the cases in the area of failure to follow the statute for adoption have proceeded on a contract theory; holding that an oral contract to adopt may be shown, but that evidence supporting the contract must be 'clear and conclusive of the existence and terms of the contract, leaving no room for reasonable doubt.' (Monahan v. Monahan, 14 Ill.2d 449, 452, 153 N.E.2d 1 (1958).) And the evidence must not be 'readily harmonizable with any other theory' than the intent to adopt. 14 Ill.2d 449, 453, 153 N.E.2d 1." *Matter of Edwards' Estate*, 106 Ill. App.3d 635, 639, 435 N.E.2d 1379 (1982). Current through P.A. 97–243, with the exception of P.A. 97–227 and P.A. 97–229, of the 2011 Reg. Sess.
Indiana	No—Does not recognize
Iowa	IOWA CODE ANN. § 633.219 (West 2012). "A person claiming to inherit under the theory of adoption by estoppel or equitable adoption has the burden to prove (1) an unexecuted agreement or contract to adopt entered into by the decedent, and (2) performance by the adopted child." In re Estate of Thompson, 760 N.W.2d 208 (Iowa Ct. App. 2008).

State	Statutory Citations and Relevant cases
Kansas	No—Does not recognize "Rather than open our courts to the various claims available under "equitable adoption," we again decline to recognize this doctrine." Matter of Estate of Robbins, 738 P.2d 458, 463 (Kan. 1987).
Kentucky	No—Does not recognize
Louisiana	No—Does not recognize
Maine	No—Does not recognize
Maryland	MD CODE ANN., EST. AND TRUSTS § 3–104 (West 2012). "Maryland therefore recognizes the doctrine of equitable adoption as it applies to an equitably adopted child who seeks to inherit by intestate succession from the estate of an equitably adoptive parent." *Board of Educ. of Montgomery County v. Browning*, 635 A.2d 373, 378 (Md. 1994).
Massachusetts	No—Does not recognize
Michigan	MICH. COMP. LAWS ANN. § 600.861 (West 2012). "In Michigan, this doctrine has been "used to create a right of intestate succession in children where there was an effort to adopt which was ineffective due to a failure to meet statutory requirements or where there was an agreement to adopt which the parent failed to perform". *The Travelers Ins. Co. v. Young,* 580 F.Supp. 421, 423 (E.D.Mich.1984). Whether there was an agreement to adopt must be decided on all the facts and circumstances of the case and an agreement may be inferred even in the absence of direct proof. *Perry v. Boyce,* 323 Mich. 95, 100–101, 34 N.W.2d 570 (1948)." Matter of Estate of Crossman, 377 N.W.2d

State	Statutory Citations and Relevant cases
	850, 853 (Mich. Ct. App. 1985) (citation omitted).
Minnesota	"Appellants do not cite, and we have not found, any Minnesota case that applies the doctrine of equitable adoption in any context other than inheritance. The district court declined to apply the doctrine in this child-support case, and we also decline to extend the application of the doctrine to circumstances under which it has not previously been applied. *See Northfield Ins. Co. v. St. Paul Surplus Lines Ins. Co.,* 545 N.W.2d 57, 62 (Minn.App.1996) ("The Minnesota Supreme Court is the appropriate forum to address a question regarding the extension of existing law." (quotation omitted)), *review denied* (Minn. June 19, 1996); *Tereault v. Palmer,* 413 N.W.2d 283, 286 (Minn. App.1987) (stating that "the task of extending existing law falls to the supreme court or the legislature, but it does not fall to this court")." *Ramsey County v. Yee Lee*, 770 N.W.2d 572, 580 (Minn. Ct. App. 2009).
Mississippi	No—Does not recognize
Missouri	Mo. ANN. STAT. § 453.090 (West 2011). No—Does not recognize "For the foregoing reasons, we hold that the legislature did not intend to preclude an equitably adopted child from bringing a wrongful death action and that allowing the action furthers the purposes of the statute and is consistent with *O'Grady v. Brown, supra.* James Holt, the decreed equitably adopted child in this case, is an adopted child under § 537.080(1)." *Holt v. Burlington N. R. Co.*, 685 S.W.2d 851, 859 (Mo. Ct. App. 1984).
Montana	No—Does not recognize

State	Statutory Citations and Relevant cases
	"[A]lthough Montana does recognize the doctrine of equitable adoption in estate cases, the grant of relief in equity does not undertake to change the legal status of the stepchild from a contract claimant to an "heir" of the decedent. Therefore, since the child had not legally been adopted, he was not entitled to the state inheritance tax exemption afforded the child of the deceased." *Pierce v. Pierce*, 645 P.2d 1353, 1355 (Mont. 1982).
Nebraska	No—Does not recognize
	"Adoption proceedings do not depend upon equitable principles, and where essential statutory requirements have not been met, equity cannot decree an adoption. Neb. Rev. Stat. 1943, § 43–101 (1943)." *Appeal of Ritchie*, 53 N.W.2d 753, 757 (Neb. 1952).
Nevada	Nev. Rev. Stat. § 41.085 (2011).
	"[W]e see no justification for refusing to extend the principles of equitable adoption so as to entitle the subject thereof to maintain an action for the wrongful death of his adoptive parents." *Bower v. Landa*, 371 P.2d 657, 661 (Nev. 1962).
New Hampshire	No—Does not recognize
New Jersey	N.J. Stat. Ann. § 9:3–50 (2012).
	"It is now firmly established that an oral agreement to adopt, where there has been a full and faithful performance on the part of the adoptive child, but which was never consummated by formal adoption proceedings during the life of the adoptive parent, will, upon the death of the latter, and when equity and justice so requires, be enforced to the extent of decreeing that such child occupies in equity the status of an adopted child, entitled to the same right of inheritance from so

State	Statutory Citations and Relevant cases
	much of his foster parent's estate that remains undisposed of by will or otherwise, as he would have been had he been a natural born child." *D'Accardi v. Chater*, 96 F.3d 97, 100 (4th Cir. 1996).
New Mexico	N.M. STAT. ANN. § 40–4–11.1 (West 2011). "In our view, the district court extended the application of the equitable adoption doctrine beyond its intended scope. We are unpersuaded that the doctrine should be expanded to child support under these circumstances. We are also unpersuaded that Bowdoin has any standing to assert the doctrine for his own benefit. Even were the doctrine to be extended to the child support context, the doctrine must be asserted by or on behalf of the child, not by the biological father for his own benefit." *Poncho v. Bowdoin,* 2006–NMCA–013, 138 N.M. 857, 866, 126 P.3d 1221, 1230.
New York	N.Y. EST. POWERS & TRUSTS LAW § 4–1.1 (McKinney 2011). "Equitable adoption is a doctrine of law that is recognized in this State (*Middleworth v. Ordway,* 191 N.Y. 404, 84 N.E. 291) . . . This doctrine does not create a legal adoption by the decedent of the child, but is merely an exercise of the court's equitable powers whereby a child is permitted to enforce the agreement to adopt made by the decedent and thereby acquire the rights in intestacy that he would have had if the decedent had complied with the said agreement." *Rodriguez v. Morris*, 136 Misc. 2d 103, 105, 519 N.Y.S.2d 451, 453 (Sur. 1987) (alteration in original).
North Carolina	N.C. GEN. STAT. ANN. § 48–3–100 (West 2011).

State	Statutory Citations and Relevant cases
	"Equitable adoption, however, does not confer the incidents of formal statutory adoption; rather, it merely confers rights of inheritance upon the foster child in the event of intestacy of the foster parents." *Lankford v. Wright*, 347 N.C. 115, 118, 489 S.E.2d 604, 606 (1997)
North Dakota	N.D. CENT. CODE § 31–11–05 (Supp. 2011). "As indicated, equitable adoption has been recognized in this state, but its recognition has been strictly for inheritance issues where the deceased has not expressed a contrary intent by will." *Johnson v. Johnson*, 2000 ND 170, 617 N.W.2d 97, 113.
Ohio	No—Does not recognize "Furthermore, we decline to expand to the law of inheritance the very limited and narrow application of the doctrine of 'equitable adoption,' espoused by the sisters and enunciated in *Lawson v. Atwood* (1989), 42 Ohio St.3d 69, 71–72, 536 N.E.2d 1167, 1169" *York v. Nunley*, 610 N.E.2d 576, 578 (Ohio Ct. App. 1992).
Oklahoma	"To assert a claim of equitable adoption, Plaintiff must show that a binding contract between himself and a natural parent of the child existed prior to the expiration of the specified time. The fact question which the Examiner faced was whether a contract for adoption existed. The standard of proof is that the contract must be established by clear and convincing evidence." *Crozier v. Cohen*, 299 F. Supp. 563, 565 (W.D. Okla. 1969).
Oregon	Does not permit a child to acquire such rights under the theory of equitable adoption if the contract to adopt was entered into in that State. However,

State	Statutory Citations and Relevant cases
	such contracts made in another State will be enforced if valid and enforceable in that State. See *In re Schultz' Estate,* 348 P.2d 22, 27 (Or. 1959).
Pennsylvania	No—Does not recognize See *Benson v. Nicholas,* 98 A. 775 (Pa. 1916).
Rhode Island	"The doctrine has gradually been incorporated into tort law and was recognized by the Rhode Island Superior Court in *Francois v. Cahill.* According to the Superior Court in *Francois,* the five elements required to establish an equitable adoption are: 1. some showing of an agreement between the adoptive parent and the natural parents; 2. the natural parents giving custody of the child to the adoptive parent; 3. the child giving filial affection, devotion and obedience to the adoptive parent during that parent's lifetime; 4. the adoptive parent taking custody of the child and treating that child as the parent's natural child; and, 5. the death of the adoptive parent without the completion of formal adoption procedures." *Crawford v. Cooper/T. Smith Stevedoring Co., Inc.,* 14 F. Supp. 2d 202, 212 (D.R.I. 1998).
South Carolina	S.C. CODE ANN. § 63–9–20 (West 2012). No—Does not recognize "The adoption of a child was a proceeding unknown to the common law and exists only by virtue of statutory authority which expressly prescribes the conditions under which an adoption may legally be effected; the method of adoption provided by statute is exclusive. Thus, a trial judge's order finding that a de facto or equitable adoption had occurred would be re-

State	Statutory Citations and Relevant cases
	versed." Alley v. Bennett, 379 S.E.2d 294, 296 (S.C. App. 1989). Current through End of 2010 Reg. Sess.
South Dakota	"[T]his court reaffirmed its adherence to the rule that one claiming the benefit of an alleged contract for adoption has the burden of establishing it by evidence so clear, cogent and convincing as to leave no reasonable doubt as to the agreement." Crilly v. Morris, 19 N.W.2d 836, 843 (S.D. 1945).
Tennessee	Tenn. Code Ann. § 36–1–121 (2012). No—Does not recognize "As against the adopted child the statute must be strictly construed because it is in derogation of the general law of inheritance, which general law of inheritance is founded on natural relationships, is a rule of succession according to nature, and has prevailed from time immemorial." *Delamotte v. Stout*, 340 S.W.2d 894, 895 (Tenn. 1960).
Texas	Tex. Prob. Code Ann. § 40 (2011). "The descriptive phrases, 'equitable adoption,' 'adoption by estoppel,' and 'adoptive status,' are used in decided cases strictly as a shorthand method of saying that because of the promises, acts and conduct of an intestate deceased, those claiming under and through him are estopped to assert that a child was not legally adopted or did not occupy the status of an adopted child." *Heien v. Crabtree*, 369 S.W.2d 28, 30 (Tex. 1963).
Utah	No—Does not recognize
Vermont	Vt. Stat. Ann. tit. 14 § 1492 (2012). "Courts generally apply the doctrine of equitable adoption in cases of intestate

State	Statutory Citations and Relevant cases
	succession to permit participation in the estate by a foster child who was never legally ... adopted by the decedent. Typically the decedent obtained custody by expressly or implicitly promising the child, the child's natural parents, or someone In loco parentis that an adoption would occur." *Whitchurch v. Perry*, 408 A.2d 627, 631 (Vt. 1979).
Virginia	No—Does not recognize
Washington	No—Does not recognize
	"Not having been adopted by Benjamin in the manner required by our adoption statutes, and there never having been recognized in this state any lawful method of adoption other than by sanction of a probate court in territorial days, or of a superior court since the beginning of statehood, evidenced by decree or order duly rendered by one or the other of such courts, Robert has no standing whatever as a legally adopted son of Benjamin." *Fields v. Fields*, 243 P. 369, 371 (Wash. 1926).
West Virginia	Wheeling Dollar Savings & Trust Co. v. Singer, 250 S.E.2d 369 (W. Va. 1978) (Recognized equitable adoption if the claimant can prove with clear, cogent and convincing proof that she was treated as and considered the adopted child of the decedent).
Wisconsin	No—Does not recognize
Wyoming	Wyo. Stat. Ann. § 1–22–114 (2011).
	"The primary function of equitable adoption is to enforce a child's right to inherit from someone who promised, but failed, to adopt that child, and then died intestate." *In re Estate of Seader*, 2003 WY 119, 76 P.3d 1236, 1245 (Wyo. 2003).

VI. Inheritance and Adoption

The aim of state adoption statutes is to treat the adopted child as if the child were the natural-born child of the adoptive parents. For the vast majority of states that goal is achieved through inheritance statutes. Treating an adopted child as a natural child of the adoptive parents poses questions for rights of inheritance for all of the parties involved.

For all but six states, upon the decree of adoption, the adopted child no longer inherits from his biological relatives. In the states allowing continued inheritance through the biological relatives, the adopted child is permitted only to inherit from his natural parents but is treated as the child of the adoptive parents, including the additional right to inherit through the adoptive parents as well.

However, for the reverse question of whether or not biological relatives inherit through the adopted child, Wyoming is the only state which permits the biological relatives to inherit through the child; all other states prohibit the biological relatives from inheriting through the adopted child. Wyoming, however, considers the adopted child to be the child of the natural parents and the adopted parents solely for inheritance purposes. WYO. STAT. § 2–4–107.

In keeping with the tendency to treat the adopted child as the natural-born child of the adoptive parents, the adopted child inherits through its adoptive relatives in every state. Additionally, the adoptive parents inherit through the adopted children in every state.

When a child is adopted by a step-parent, its parental relationship with the spouse of that step-parent (the child's natural parent) is typically unaffected. However, the effect that the adoption has on the adopted child's inheritance relationship with the other natural parent is state specific and may in fact depend on whether or not the other natural parent was deceased before the decree of adoption.

The following charts are organized by asking three questions: (1) Does an adopted child inherit from his/her biological relatives; (2) Do biological relatives inherit from the adopted child; (3) Does the adopted child inherit from his/her adopted relatives; (4) Do adopted relatives inherit from the adopted child?

A. Question One: Does an Adopted Child Inherit From His/Her Biological Relatives?

1. States Answering This Question No

State	UPC	Statute	Answer
Alabama	Yes	ALA. CODE § 43–8–48 (2012).	No.
Alaska	Yes	Alaska Stat. §§ 13.12.114; 25.23.130 (2012).	No.
Arizona	Yes	ARIZ. REV. STAT. ANN. §§ 8–117(B); 14–2109 (2012).	No.
Arkansas	No	ARK. STAT. ANN. § 9–9–215 (2011).	No.

State	UPC	Statute	Answer
California	No	CAL. PROB. CODE §§ 6451(a); 257 (2012).	No. (a) No parent child relationship between adoptee and biological parent for purposes of intestate succession; exception: stepparent rule of (1) relationship began during the child's minority and continued through the parties' joint lifetimes and (2) clear and convincing evidence that the stepparent would have adopted the person but for a legal barrier.
Colorado	No	COLO. REV. STAT. §§ 15–11–103; 15–11–114 (2012).	No. Except narrow circumstances . . . if an adopted individual is the child of the adopter and not the birth parents except that if the birth parent dies without other surviving descendents, parents, grandparents, or descendants of parents or grandparents, then the birth child inherits the estate.
Connecticut	No	CONN. GEN. STAT. ANN. § 45a–731(5–6) (2012).	No. Legal relationship between adoptee and biological parents and relatives is terminated for all purposes, including inheritance.
Delaware	Yes	DEL. CODE ANN. tit. 12 §§ 508, 919; tit 13, § 920(a) (2011).	No. Effect of adoption on rights in general: adoptee no longer the child of the biological parent or parents; and not entitled to any rights with respect to biological parents . . . § 920(a) . . . rights of inheritance between adop-

State	UPC	Statute	Answer
			tee and biological parent or parents and their relatives cease.
District of Columbia	No	D.C. CODE ANN. § 16–312 (2012).	No. All rights of inheritance and succession between adoptee and biological parents, their issue, and collateral relatives are terminated.
Florida	No	FLA. STAT. ANN. §§ 63.172(1)(b); 732.108 (2012).	No. Adoption terminates all inheritance rights between adoptee and biological relatives, including biological parents.
Georgia	No	GA. CODE. ANN. § 19–8–19 (2011).	No.
Hawaii	Yes	HAW. REV. STAT. §§ 560:2–109; 578–16* (2011).	No. For purposes of descent of property, biological parents and biological relatives [are] not considered related to adoptee.
Idaho	No	IDAHO CODE ANN. § 16–1509 (2012).	No. Adoptee loses right to inherit from and through biological parents.
Indiana	No	IND. CODE ANN. § 29–1–2–8 (2011).	No. For all purposes of intestate succession, including succession by, through or from a person, adoption terminates relationship between child and biological parents or any previous adopting parents.
Iowa	No	IOWA CODE § 633.223.1 (2012).	No. Adoption extinguishes the right of intestate succession of biological parent from and through biological parents.
Kentucky	No	KY. REV. STAT. ANN. § 199.520(2) (2011).	No. Adoption terminates legal relationship between the adoptee and birth parents. It follows from this rule that

State	UPC	Statute	Answer
			there is no inheritance between an adoptee and biological parents or other members of the biological family.
Maine	Yes	ME. REV. STAT. ANN. tit. 18–A § 2–109 (2011).	No. <u>Unless</u> the adoption decree so specifies.
Maryland	No	MD. CODE ANN., EST. & TRUSTS § 1–207(a) (2012); MD. CODE ANN., FAM. LAW § 5–3B–25 (2012).	No. Adoptee is no longer considered the child of either natural parent.
Massachusetts	Yes	MASS. GEN. LAWS ANN. ch. 210 § 7** (West 2012).	No. Adoptee loses right to inherit from biological parents and relatives.
Michigan	No	MICH. COMP. LAWS ANN. § 710.60(2) (West 2012).	No. On adoption, adoptee is no longer heir of biological parents or other biological relatives
Minnesota	No	MINN. STAT. ANN. § 259.59 (West 2012).	No. Adoptee does not inherit from natural parents or kindred . . . this is the case even if the adoption occurred at a time when the law permitted an adoptee to inherit from the biological family . . . the governing principle is that the right to inherit does not vest until the biological relative's death, and if the death postdates the enactment of the current statute, which denies an adoptee the right to inherit from biological relatives, then there can be no right to inherit. *In re estate of Carlson*; 457 N.W.2d 789

State	UPC	Statute	Answer
Mississippi	No	No statutory provision addresses this question. Relevant case law: *Alack v. Phelps*, 230 So.2d 789 (Miss. 1970); *Fairchild Constr. Co. v. Owens*, 224 So.2d 571 (Miss. 1969).	No. No statutory provision addresses this point; one court examining this question observed that while adoption terminated the right of the biological parents to inherit through an adoptee, the relevant statute did not state that the right of the child to inherit from the biological parents is to be terminated; thus indicating a legislative intent to preserve the child's right. (*Alack v. Phelps*; 230 So.2d 789). In a case involving a claim for worker's compensation benefits, by contrast, the court found a legislative intent to sever all rights, duties and obligations of the biological parent towards the adoptee (*W.R. Fairchild Constr. Co. v. Owens*, 224 So.2d 571). The court denied the claim on the grounds that the benefit sought involved a statutory entitlement rather than an inheritance right, and held that the adoption terminated the right to benefit.
Missouri	Yes	MO. ANN. STAT. §§ 474.060; 453.090.1 (2011).	No. Terminating all legal relationships rights and duties between adoptee and biological parents.
Montana	Yes	MONT. CODE ANN. § 72–2–124	No. Adoptee is not child of natural par-

State	UPC	Statute	Answer
		(2011).	ent for intestate inheritance purposes.
Nebraska	Yes	NEB. REV. STAT. § 30–2309 (2011).	No.
Nevada	No	NEV. REV. STAT. § 127.160 (2011).	No. Adoptee does not inherit from natural parents or relatives of natural parents.
New Hampshire	No	N.H. REV. STAT. ANN. § 170–B:20 (2011).	No. Adoptee loses all rights of inheritance from natural parents and relatives.
New Jersey	No	N.J. STAT. ANN. § 9:3–50(c) (2012).	No. Termination of all rights of inheritance under intestacy from or through the biological parent.
New Mexico	Yes	N.M. STAT. ANN. § 45–2–114 (2011).	No.
New York	No	N.Y. DOM. REL. LAW § 117.1(b) (2011).	No. Adoptee does not inherit from or through natural parents.
North Carolina	No	N.C. GEN. STAT. § 29–17(b) (2011).	No. Adoptee does not inherit from or through natural parents or their heirs.
North Dakota	Yes	N.D. CENT. CODE §§ 30.1–04–09; 14–15–14(1)(a) (2011).	No. Adoptee is a stranger to former relatives for all purposes including inheritance.
Ohio	No	OHIO REV. CODE ANN. § 3107.15(A)(1) *** (2011).	No. Adoptee is a stranger to former relatives for all purposes including inheritance.
Oklahoma	No	No statutory provision addresses this question. Relevant case law: *In re Estate of Marriott*, 515 P.2d	No. There is no statutory provision addressing this question. Case law indicates that the adoptee retains the right to inherit from biological parents and relatives ...

State	UPC	Statute	Answer
		571 (Okla. 1973); *In re Fox*, 567 P.2d 985 (Okla. 1977).	. . . *In re Estate of Marriott* (515 P.2d 571) . . . adoptee inherits from both natural and adoptive parents. Another case, however, suggests that adoption completely transplants the inheritance relationship from the former family to the adoptive family. In re Fox (567 P. 2d 985) . . . regarding grandparent visitation rights . . . but does not directly address inheritance
Oregon	No	OR. REV. STAT. § 112.175(2) (2012).	No. Terminating parent-child relationship between adoptee and biological parents for all purposes of intestate succession by adoptee, the adoptee's issue and kindred, and the natural parents and their use of kindred.
Pennsylvania	No	20 PA. CONS. STAT. ANN. § 2108 (West 2011).	No. Except as to a biological relative (other than a parent) with whom the adoptee maintains a family relationship
South Carolina	Yes	S.C. CODE ANN. § 62-2-109 (2012).	No.
South Dakota	No	S.D. CODIFIED LAWS § 29A-2-114(b) (2012).	No. For purposes of intestate succession by, from or through a person, an adopted individual is the child of that individual's adopting parent or parents and not of that individual's birth parents, except in the

State	UPC	Statute	Answer
			case of a stepparent adoption.
Tennessee	Yes	Tenn. Code Ann. §§ 36–1–126(e); 31–2–105 (2012).	No. Adoptee does not inherit from natural parent or relatives of natural parent.
Utah	Yes	Utah Code Ann. § 75–2–109 (2011).	No. Nor is an adoptee the child of previously adopting parents for intestate succession purposes.
Vermont	No	Vt. Stat. Ann. tit. 15A, § 1–105 (2012).	No. Adoptee's right of inheritance through intestacy from or through each former parent terminates.
Virginia	Yes	Va. Code Ann. § 64.1–5.1 (2012).	No.
Washington	No	Wash. Rev. Code Ann. § 11.04.085 (2012). Relevant case law: *In re Estates of Donnelly*, 81 Wash.2d 430, 502 P.2d 1163 (1972).	No. adoptee is not an heir of biological parents for inheritance purposes. It follows from this rule that an adoptee does not inherit from other biological relatives either . . . sever all ties with the past.
West Virginia	No	W. Va. Code § 48–22–703 (2012).	No. Adoptee does not inherit from biological parents or previously adopting parents or their lineal or collateral relatives.
Wisconsin	No	Wis. Stat. Ann. §§ 854.20(2); 48.92(2) (2011).	No. Adoptee ceases to be treated as a child of natural parents for purposes of intestate succession by, through, or from the adoptee . . . adoption severs all rights, duties and legal consequences of the parent-child relationship between an adoptee and the adoptee's birth parents.

* Haw. Rev. Stat. § 578–16: proposed legislative amendment 2011
** Mass. Gen. Laws Ann. ch. 210 § 7: proposed legislative action 2011

*** OHIO REV. CODE. ANN. § 3107.15(A)(1): limited on constitutional grounds in *Bank One Trust Co. N.A. v. Reynolds*, 173 Ohio App.3d 1, 1+, 877 N.E.2d 342 (2007)

2. States Answering This Question Yes

State	UPC	Statute	Answer
Illinois	No	750 ILL. COMP. STAT. 50/17 (2011).	Yes. In re Estate of Cregar (30 Ill. App. 3d 798, 333 N.E.2d 540)
		Relevant case law: *In re Estate of Cregar*, 30 Ill App. 3d 798; Tilliski's Estate, 323 Ill. App. 490, 56 N.E.2d 481 (1945); In re M.M., 156 Ill. 2d 53, 619 N.E.2d 702 (1993).	(1975) adoption by nonrelative does not terminate adoptee's right to inherit from biological parents and biological relatives) ... In re Tilliski's Estate, 323 Ill. App. 490, 56 N.E.2d 481 (1945) ... adoptee may inherit from and through biological parent ... In re M.M., 156 Ill. 2d 53, 619 N.E.2d 702 (1993) ... adoption severs all rights between natural parents and children except parents' residual duty to support and children's right to inherit from and through the biological parent.
Kansas	No	KAN. STAT. ANN. § 59–2118(b) (2012).	Yes. An adoption shall not terminate the right of the child to inherit from or through the birth parent
Louisiana	No	LA. CIV. CODE ANN. art. 199 (2011).	Yes. Adoptee and descendants of adoptee retain right of inheritance from adoptee's biological parents and other biological relatives.

State	UPC	Statute	Answer
Rhode Island	No	R.I. GEN. LAWS § 15–7–17 (2011).	Yes. Adoptee retains right to inherit from and through natural parents.
Texas	No	TEX. PROB. CODE ANN. § 40 (2011).	Yes. Adoptee inherits from and through natural parents; Go Int'l Inc. v. Lewis, 601 S.W.2d 495.
		Relevant Case Law: *Go Int'l, Inc. v. Lewis*, 601 S.W.2d 495 (Tex. Civ.App.1980); *Ybarra v. Texas Dep't of Human Services*, 869 S.W.2d 574 (Tex. App.1993)	Ybarra v. Texas Dep't of Human Services, 869 S.W.2d. 574.
Wyoming	No	WYO. STAT. ANN. § 2–4–107 (2011).	Yes. Adoptee is child of adoptive parent and natural parent for inheritance purposes.

For the great majority of states, once the child has been adopted, the adopted child ceases to be the child of the birth parents and assumes the full rights and relationships available as if he or she were naturally born of the adopted parents. For the select few (6) states allowing inheritance through the biological relatives after the adoption decree, adopted children inherit from both the birth parents and the adoptive parents.

B. Question Two: Do Biological Relatives Inherit From Adoptee?

State	Statute	Answer
Alabama	ALA. CODE § 43–8–48 (2012).	No.
Alaska	ALASKA STAT. §§ 13.12.114;	No. Decree of adoption can provide for continua-

State	Statute	Answer
	25.23.130 (2012).	tion of inheritance rights.
Arizona	ARIZ. REV. STAT. ANN. §§ 8–117(b); 14–2109 (2012).	No.
Arkansas	ARK. CODE ANN. § 9–9–215 (2011).	No.
California	CAL. FAM. CODE § 8617 (2012); CAL. PROB. CODE § 6451(a–b) (2012).	No. Birth parents have no right over adopted child; no parent-child relationship between adoptee and biological parent for purposes of intestate succession, *except* if certain specified requirements are satisfied . . . biological parents and relatives do not inherit from or through an adoptee.
Colorado	COLO. REV. STAT. §§ 15–11–114; 19–5–211 (2012).	No. For purposes of intestate inheritance by, from or through a person, an adopted individual is the child of the adopter and not the birth parents . . . natural parents divested all legal rights and obligations concerning adoptee, and adoptee is free from legal obligations of obedience and maintenance regarding natural parents.
Connecticut	CONN. GEN. STAT. ANN. § 45a–731(5–6) (West 2012).	No. Legal relationship between adoptee and biological parents and relatives is terminated for all purposes, including inheritance.
Delaware	DEL. CODE. ANN. tit. 12 § 508;	No. Rights of inheritance between adoptee and bio-

State	Statute	Answer
	13, § 920(a) (2011).	logical parents or parents and their relatives cease.
District of Columbia	D.C. CODE § 16–312 (2012).	No. All rights of inheritance and succession between adoptee and biological parents, their issue, and collateral relatives are terminated.
Florida	FLA. STAT. ANN. §§ 63.172(1)(b); 732.108 (2012).	No. Adoption terminates rights between adoptee and biological relatives, including biological parents.
Georgia	GA. CODE. ANN. § 19–8–19 (2011).	No.
Hawaii	HAW. REV. STAT. §§ 560:2–109; 578–16 (2011).	No. For purposes of descent of property, biological parents and biological relatives [are] not considered related to adoptee.
Idaho	IDAHO CODE ANN. § 16–1509 (2012).	No. At least with respect to biological parents . . . biological parents have no right over adopted child. Although the statute does not make any specific reference to other biological relatives, it is safe to assume that adoption terminates other relatives' rights to inherit as well.
Illinois	755 ILL. COMP. STAT. 5/2–4(b)** (2011).	No, except with respect to property the adoptee has taken from or through the biological parent or biological relatives by gift, will, or under intestate laws . . . natural parent and lineal and collateral kindred of natural parent do not inherit from adoptee, except to the extent noted.

State	Statute	Answer
Indiana	IND. CODE ANN. § 29–1–2–8 (2011).	No. For all purposes of intestate succession, including succession by, through or from a person, adoption terminates relationship between child and biological parents or any previous adopting parents.
Iowa	IOWA CODE § 633.223.2 (2012).	No. Adoption extinguishes the right of intestate succession of biological parent from and through adoptee. Note that the statute does not address the rights of biological relatives to inherit, though looking at § 663.223.3, indicates that biological relatives' rights to inherit are also terminated upon adoption.
Kansas	KAN. STAT. ANN. § 59–2118 (2011).	No. Birth parents' right to inherit is terminated. Although the statute does not make a specific reference to the rights of relatives to inherits, it is safe to assume that biological relatives' rights to inherit is also terminated upon adoption.
Kentucky	KY. REV. STAT. ANN. § 199.520(2) (2011).	No. Adoption terminates all legal relationship between the adoptee and birth parents. It follows from this rule that there is no inheritance between an adoptee and biological parents or other members of the biological family.
Louisiana	LA. CHILD. CODE art. 1218, 1240 (2011).	No. Biological parents and biological relatives divested of right of inheri-

State	Statute	Answer
		tance from adoptee and descendents of adoptee.
Maine	Me. Rev. Stat. Ann. tit. 18–A § 2–109; 18–A, § 9–105 (2011).	No.
Maryland	Md. Code Ann., Est. & Trusts § 1–207(a) (2012); Md. Code Ann., Fam. Law § 5–3B–25 (2012).	No. Inheritance between adoptee and natural relatives is governed by Est. and Trust Code provision . . . it follows from this rule that the adoptee inherits from neither the biological parents nor biological relatives. . . . and vice versa.
Massachusetts	Mass. Gen. Laws Ann. ch. 210 § 7 (West 2012).	No.
Michigan	Mich. Comp. Laws Ann. §§ 700.2114 (4); 710.60(2) (2012).	No. Inheritance through adopted child by natural parent or kindred is precluded unless that natural parent has treated the child as his/hers and not refused child support.
Minnesota	Minn. Stat. Ann. § 259.59 (West 2012).	No. Natural parents have no rights over adoptee's property. Although the statute does not specifically mention the rights of biological relatives, it can be argue by inference that the other biological relatives' inheritance rights are also terminated.
Mississippi	Miss. Code Ann. § 93–17–13% (2011).	No. Biological parents and relatives do not inherit by or through adoptee.
Missouri	Mo. Ann. Stat. §§ 474.060;	No. Terminating all legal relationships rights and

State	Statute	Answer
	453.090.1 (2011).	duties between adoptee and biological parents
Montana	Mont. Code Ann. §§ 72–2–124; 42–5–202 (2011).	No. Inheritance through adopted child by natural parent or kindred is precluded unless that natural parent has treated the child as his/hers and not refused child support.
Nebraska	Neb. Rev. Stat. §§ 30–2309; 43–111; 43–106.01 (2011).	No. Natural parents have no inheritance rights vis-à-vis adoptee . . . parent who relinquishes child to government or placement agency has no rights over child.
Nevada	Nev. Rev. Stat. § 127.160 (2011).	No. Natural parents have no rights over child's property. The statute fails to specifically address the rights of biological relatives to inherit from the adoptee, however by inference and analogy, it is safe to assume that their rights to inherit will also be precluded.
New Hampshire	N.H. Rev. Stat. Ann. § 170–B:20 (2011).	No. Natural parents and their relatives do not inherit from adoptee.
New Jersey	N.J. Stat. Ann. § 9:3–50(c) (2012).	No. Termination of all rights of inheritance under intestacy that existed before adoption from or through the child.
New Mexico	N.M. Stat. Ann. § 45–2–114 (2011).	No.
New York	N.Y. Dom. Rel. Law § 117.1(a) (2011).	No. Natural parents' inheritance rights are terminated. The statute fails to specifically address the rights of biological relatives to inherit from the adoptee, however by in-

State	Statute	Answer
		ference and analogy, it is safe to assume that their rights to inherit will also be precluded. See Also In re Trainor's Estate; 45 Misc.2d 316, 256 N.Y.S.2d 497.
North Carolina	N.C. GEN. STAT. §§ 29–17(d); 48–1–106 (2011).	No. Natural parents and their heirs do not inherit from or through adoptee . . . biological parents divested of all rights with respect to adoptee.
North Dakota	N.D. CENT. CODE §§ 30.1–04–09; 14–15–14(1)(a) (2011).	No. Adoptee is stranger to formal relatives for all purposes.
Ohio	OHIO REV. CODE ANN. § 3107.15 (A)(1)^ (2011).	No. Adoptee is stranger to former relatives for all purposes.
Oklahoma	OKLA. STAT. ANN. tit. 10, § 7505–6.5 (2011).	No. Natural parents do not inherit from adoptee. The statute fails to specifically address the rights of biological relatives to inherit from the adoptee, however by inference and analogy, it is safe to assume that their rights to inherit will also be precluded.
Oregon	OR. REV. STAT. § 112.175(2) (2012).	No. Terminating parent-child relationship between adoptee and biological parents for all purposes of intestate succession by adoptee, the adoptee's issue and kindred, and the natural parents and their issue and kindred.
Pennsylvania	20 PA. CONS. STAT. ANN. § 2108 (West 2011).	No, except as to a biological relative with whom the adoptee maintains a family relationship . . .

State	Statute	Answer
		this is in respect of an adoptee inheriting from a biological relative. The statute fails to specifically address the rights of biological relatives to inherit from the adoptee, however by inference and analogy, it is safe to assume that their rights to inherit will also be subject to the same exception mentioned above.
Rhode Island	R.I. GEN. LAWS § 15–7–17 (2011).	No. Natural parents are deprived of all legal rights with respect to adoptee. The statute fails to specifically address the rights of biological relatives to inherit from the adoptee, however by inference and analogy, it is safe to assume that their rights to inherit will also be precluded.
South Carolina	S.C. CODE ANN. §§ 62–2–109; 20–7–1770 (2012).	No. Natural parents have no rights over adoptee. The statute fails to specifically address the rights of biological relatives to inherit from the adoptee, however by inference and analogy, it is safe to assume that their rights to inherit will also be precluded.
South Dakota	S.D. CODIFIED LAWS §§ 25–6–17; 29A–2–114(b) (2012).	No. Natural parents have no rights over adoptee. The statute fails to specifically address the rights of biological relatives to inherit from the adoptee, however by inference and analogy, it is safe to assume that their rights to

State	Statute	Answer
		inherit will also be precluded.
Tennessee	TENN. CODE ANN. §§ 31–2–105; 36–1–121(e)****** (2012).	No. Natural parent and relatives of natural parent do not inherit from adoptee.
Texas	TEX. PROB. CODE ANN. § 40 (2011).	No. Natural parents and their relatives do not inherit from or through adoptee ... divested of all rights with respect to adoptee.
Utah	UTAH CODE. ANN. §§ 75–2–114; 78B–6–138 (2011).	No. Natural parents have no rights with respect to adoptee.
Vermont	VT. STAT. ANN. tit. 15A § 1–104 (2012).	No. Biological relatives do not inherit from or through adoptee.
Virginia	VA. CODE ANN. §§ 63.2–1215; 64.1–5.1 (2012).	No. Parents and parents by previous adoption are divested of all legal rights with respect to adoptee.
Washington	WASH. REV. CODE ANN. § 26.33.260 (2012).	No. Adoption divests biological parents of all legal rights in connection with adoptee. The statute fails to specifically address the rights of biological relatives to inherit from the adoptee, however by inference and analogy, it is safe to assume that their rights to inherit will also be precluded. (See In re Estates of Donnelly (81 Wash.2d 430)).
West Virginia	W. VA. CODE § 48–22–703 (2012).	No. Biological parents or previously adopting parents, and their lineal or collateral kindred, are divested of all rights to inherit from adoptee.

State	Statute	Answer
Wisconsin	WIS. STAT. ANN. §§ 854.20(2); 48.92(2) (2011).	No. Adoptee ceases to be treated as child of natural parents for purposes of intestate succession by, through or from the adoptee; adoption severs all rights, duties and legal consequences of the parent-child relationship between adoptee and the adoptee's birth parents.
Wyoming	WYO. STAT. ANN. § 2–4–107 (2011).	Yes. The adoptee is child of adoptive parent and natural parent for inheritance purposes

* HAW. REV. STAT. § 578–16: proposed legislative amendment 2011

** 755 ILL. COMP. STAT. 5/2–4: proposed legislative amendment 2011

*** MASS. GEN. LAWS ANN. ch. 210, § 7: proposed legislative action 2011

**** MICH. COMP. LAWS § 700.2114(4): proposed legislative amendment 2011

***** MISS. CODE ANN. § 93–17–13: proposed legislative amendment 2011

****** TENN. CODE ANN. § 36–1–121(e): proposed legislative amendment 2011

******* UTAH CODE ANN. § 78B–6–138: proposed legislative amendment 2012

^ OHIO REV. CODE. ANN. § 3107.15(A)(1): limited on constitutional grounds in *Bank One Trust Co. N.A. v. Reynolds*, 173 Ohio App.3d 1, 1+, 877 N.E.2d 342 (2007)

For all states, except Wyoming, the biological parents and relatives are precluded from inheriting from and through the adopted child. This extends even to the states which allowed inheritance by the child from and through the biological parents. In Wyoming, the child is treated as the child of both the biological parents and the adopted parents for inheritance purposes, extending the right of inheritance to both parties.

C. Question Three: Does Adoptee Inherit From Adoptive Relatives?

State	Statute	Answer
Alabama	ALA. CODE §§ 43–8–48; 26–10A–29 (2012). Relevant Case Law: *McClure v. Noble*, 602 So.2d 377 (Ala. 1992)	Yes. Language limited to discussion of adoptee's treatment as a "natural child" of the adopting parents for purposes of inheritance, without discussing any reciprocal rights on the part of the adopting parent or extended family ... adopted children entitled to inherit from intestate collateral relatives of predeceased adoptive parents (McClure v. Noble; 602 So.2d 377)
Alaska	ALASKA STAT. § 25.23.130 (2012).	Yes.
Arizona	ARIZ. REV. STAT. ANN. §§ 8–117(b); 14–2109 (2012).	Yes. All legal consequences of parent-child relationship exist between adoptee and adoptive parent; adopted child inherits from and through adoptive parents.
Arkansas	ARK. CODE ANN. § 9–9–215 (2011).	Yes. Adoption creates a parent-child relationship between adoptee and adoptive parent for all purposes, including inheritance.
California	CAL. FAM. CODE § 8616 (2012); CAL. PROB. CODE § 6450(b) (2012).	Yes. Parent child relationship exists between adoptee and adopter, who have all the rights relative with that relationship ... parent child relationship exists between adoptee and adoptive par-

State	Statute	Answer
		ent for purposes of determining intestate succession, by, through, or from a person.
Colorado	COLO. REV. STAT. §§ 15–11–109; 19–5–211 (2012).	Yes. Adoptee is child of adoptive parents for all inheritance purposes.
Connecticut	CONN. GEN. STAT. ANN. § 45a–731(1)–(3) (West 2012).	Yes. Parent child relationship exists between adoptee and adoptive parents for all purposes, including rights of inheritance between adoptee and adoptee's heirs, on the one hand, and adoptive parents and their issue and other relatives, on the other.
Delaware	DEL. CODE. ANN. tit. 12 § 508; tit. 13 §§ 919, 920(b) (2011).	Yes. Effect of adoption on rights in general: adoptee is the child of the adoptive parent or parents, and is entitled to the same rights as if born into the adopted family. Adoptee inherits from adoptive parents and collateral or lineal relatives of the adoptive parent.
District of Columbia	D.C. CODE § 16–312 (2012).	Yes. Parent-child relationship exists between adoptee and adopter for all purpose, including mutual rights of inheritance and succession.
Florida	FLA. STAT. ANN. §§ 63.172(1)(c); 732.108 (2012).	Yes. Adoption creates the inheritance relationship between adoptee and adopter and all relatives of adopter that would have existed if the adoptee were a legitimate blood descendent of the adopter . . . adoptee is lin-

State	Statute	Answer
		eal descendent of adopter and is one of the natural kindred of all members of the adopter's family for intestate inheritance purposes.
Georgia	GA. CODE. ANN. § 19–8–19 (2011).	Yes.
Hawaii	HAW. REV. STAT. §§ 560:2–109; 578–16* (2011).	Yes.
Idaho	IDAHO CODE ANN. § 16–1508 (2012).	Yes. Adoptee inherits as if born into adoptive family.
Illinois	755 ILL. COMP. STAT. 5/2–4(a)** (2011).	Yes. Adoptee is descendent of adoptive parent for purposes of inheritance from adoptive parent and adoptive relatives.
Indiana	IND. CODE ANN. § 29–1–2–8 (2011).	Yes. For all purposes of intestate succession, including succession by, through or from a person, adoptee is treated as biological child of adopting parents.
Iowa	IOWA CODE § 633.223.1 (2012).	Yes. Adoptee inherits from and through adoptive parents.
Kansas	KAN. STAT. ANN. § 59–2118 (2011).	Yes. Adoptee has same inheritance rights as a birth child of the adoptive parents.
Kentucky	KY. REV. STAT. ANN. § 199.520(2) (2011).	Yes. Adoptee is deemed the child of the adoptive parents for all purposes of intestate inheritance.
Louisiana	LA. CHILD. CODE art. 1218, 1240 (2011).	Yes. Adoptee and descendants of adoptee inherit from the adoptive parents and adoptive relatives.

State	Statute	Answer
Maine	ME. REV. STAT. ANN. tit. 18–A §§ 2–109, 9–105 (2011).	Yes.
Maryland	MD. CODE ANN., EST. & TRUSTS § 1–207(a) (2012); MD. CODE ANN., FAM. LAW § 5–3B–25 (2012).	Yes. Adoptee is treated as a biological child of the adopting parent or parents . . . adoptee is child of adopter for all purposes.
Massachusetts	MASS. GEN. LAWS ANN. ch. 210 § 7*** (West 2012).	Yes. Adoptee inherits from both adoptive parents and from other adoptive relatives.
Michigan	MICH. COMP. LAWS ANN. §§ 700.2114 (4)****; 710.60(2) (2012).	Yes. Adoptee is heir of adoptive parents and their relatives . . . adoptee is the kindred of adopting parents for all purposes of intestate succession.
Minnesota	MINN. STAT. ANN. § 259.59 (West 2012). Relevant case law: In re Herrick's Estate, 124 Minn. 85, 144 N.W. 455 (1913)	Yes. Adoptee inherits from adoptive parents and their relatives . . . an adoptee's issue also inherit from the adopting parents.
Mississippi	MISS. CODE ANN. § 93–17–13***** (2011).	Yes. Adoptee inherits from and through adoptive parents and from other children of the adoptive parents.
Missouri	MO. ANN. STAT. §§ 474.060; 453.090.2 (2011).	Yes. Adoptee inherits from, and as child of, adoptive parents.
Montana	MONT. CODE ANN. §§ 72–2–124; 42–5–202 (2011).	Yes. All legal consequences of parent-child relationship shall exist between adoptee and

State	Statute	Answer
		adopted parents and their kindred
Nebraska	NEB. REV. STAT. §§ 30–2309; 43–110 (2011).	Yes. All rights, duties and legal consequences of parent-child relationship exist between adoptee and adoptive parents.
Nevada	NEV. REV. STAT. §§ 127.160; 134.190 (2011).	Yes. Adoptee inherits from adoptive parents and relatives . . . succession statute scheme provides that adoptees and adoptive parents and relatives inherit as provided in statute.
New Hampshire	N.H. REV. STAT. ANN. § 170–B:20 (2011).	Yes. Adoptee inherits from adoptive parents and relatives.
New Jersey	N.J. STAT. ANN. § 9:3–50(b) (2012).	Yes. Adoptee has same rights of inheritance as if born to adoptive parent.
New Mexico	N.M. STAT. ANN. §§ 45–2–114; 32A–5–37 (2011).	Yes. Adoptee inherits from and through adoptive parent.
New York	N.Y. DOM. REL. LAW § 117.1(a), (f) (2011).	Yes. Adoptee and adoptive parents inherit from and through each other and the natural and adopted relatives of the adoptive parent. An adoptee's descendents inherit through the adoptee, and thus inherit from the adoptive relatives. Also, the statute provides that an adoptee and adoptive siblings inherit from each other.
North Carolina	N.C. GEN. STAT. §§ 29–17(a); 48–1–106 (2011).	Yes. Adoptee and heirs of adoptee inherit from and through adoptive parents and their heirs . . . adop-

State	Statute	Answer
		tee inherits from and through adoptive parents.
North Dakota	N.D. CENT. CODE §§ 30.1–04–09; 14–15–14(1)(a) (2011).	Yes. Adoption creates parent-child relationship between adoptee and adoptive parent for all purposes including inheritance.
Ohio	OHIO REV. CODE ANN. § 3107.15 (A)(2)^ (2011).	Yes. Adoption creates parent-child relationship between the adoptee and adoptive parent for all purposes including inheritance.
Oklahoma	OKLA. STAT. ANN. tit. 10, § 7505–6.5 (2011).	Yes. Adoptee inherits from and through adoptive parents.
Oregon	OR. REV. STAT. § 112.175(1) (2012).	Yes. Adoptee and issue and kindred of adoptee take by intestate succession from adoptive parents and their issue and kindred.
Pennsylvania	20 PA. CONS. STAT. ANN. § 2108 (West 2011).	Yes. Adoptee is the issue of the adoptive parent for purposes of inheritance.
Rhode Island	R.I. GEN. LAWS § 15–7–16 (2011).	Yes. Adoptee and descendants of adoptee inherit from adoptive parents and their lineal and collateral kindred.
South Carolina	S.C. CODE ANN. § 62–2–109 (2012).	Yes.
South Dakota	S.D. CODIFIED LAWS §§ 25–6–16; 29A–2–114(b) (2012).	Yes. Parent child relationship exists between adoptee and adopter and the two have all the rights of that relation … adoptee inherits from any person related to adoptive parent as does any natural child.

State	Statute	Answer
Tennessee	TENN. CODE ANN. §§ 31–2–105; 36–1–126(b) (2012).	Yes. Adoptee and descendants of adoptee inherit from adoptive parents, their descendants, the lineal and collateral kindred of the adoptive parents, and the ancestors and descendants of such kindred . . . .
Texas	TEX. PROB. CODE ANN. § 40 (2011).	Yes. Adoptee and descendants of adoptee inherit from and through adoptive parents and their kindred . . . adoptee inherits from and through adoptive parents.
Utah	UTAH CODE. ANN. § 75–2–114 (2011).	Yes.
Vermont	VT. STAT. ANN. tit. 15A § 1–104 (2012).	Yes. The adoptee and issue of the adoptee inherit from the adoptive parents and their issue but not from other adoptive relatives.
Virginia	VA. CODE ANN. §§ 63.2–1215; 64.1–5.1 (2012).	Yes. Adoptee entitled to all rights and privileges of a child born to adoptive parents.
Washington	WASH. REV. CODE ANN. § 26.33.260 (2012).	Yes. Adoptee is the child of the adoptive parents for inheritance purposes.
West Virginia	W. VA. CODE § 48–22–703 (2012).	Yes. Adoptee inherits from and through adoptive parents and their lineal or collateral kindred.
Wisconsin	WIS. STAT. ANN. §§ 854.20(2); 48.92(1) (2011).	Yes. Adoptee is treated as natural child of his adoptive parents for purposes of intestate succession by, through, or from the adoptee. . . . all rights, duties and legal consequences of the parent-

State	Statute	Answer
		child relationship exist between the adoptee and the adoptive parents.
Wyoming	WYO. STAT. ANN. § 2–4–107 (2011).	Yes. Adoptee is child of adoptive parents for inheritance purposes ... adoptee has same rights of property as children and heirs at law of the adoptive parent.

* HAW. REV. STAT. § 578–16: proposed legislative amendment 2011

** 755 ILL. COMP. STAT. 5/2–4(a): proposed legislative amendment 2011

*** MASS. GEN. LAWS ANN. ch. 210, § 7: proposed legislative action 2011

**** MICH. COMP. LAWS ANN. § 700.2114(4): proposed legislative amendment 2011

***** MISS. CODE ANN. § 93–17–13: proposed legislative amendment 2011

^ OHIO REV. CODE. ANN. § 3107.15(A)(2): limited on constitutional grounds in *Bank One Trust Co. N.A. v. Reynolds*, 173 Ohio App.3d 1, 1+, 877 N.E.2d 342 (2007)

For all states, adopted children inherit from and through the members of their adopted family. Because the adoption decree functions to create a parent/child relationship between the adoptive parents and the child, it follows that the child would inherit as would a natural child born to the parents. However, in Vermont, while the adopted child inherits from and through his or her parents and their issue, the child does not inherit from biological relatives of those parents.

D. Question Four: Do Adoptive Relatives Inherit From Adoptee?

State	Statute	Answer
Alabama	ALA. CODE §§ 43–8–48; 26–10A–29 (2012).	Yes. At least with respect to adoptive parents. The statute does not discuss extended family's rights to inherit from an adopted child; however, by virtue of reason and inference, it is likely that the adoptive relatives would also likely be able to inherit from the adopted child as well.
Alaska	ALASKA STAT. § 25.23.130 (2012).	Yes.
Arizona	ARIZ. REV. STAT. ANN. §§ 8–117(a); 14–2109 (2012).	Yes. Adoptive parent inherits from and through adoptee; there is no explicit mentioning of adoptive relatives' right to inherit, however the statute does indicate that adoptive relatives would also inherit from adoptee.
Arkansas	ARK. CODE ANN. § 9–9–215 (2011).	Yes. Adoption creates parent-child relationship between adoptee and adoptive parent for all purposes, including inheritance.
California	CAL. FAM. CODE § 8616 (2012); CAL. PROB. CODE § 6450(b) (2012).	Yes. Parent-child relationship exists between adoptee and adopter, who have all the rights relative with that relationship . . . parent child relationship exists between adoptee and adoptive parent for purposes of determining intestate succession by, through, or from a person.

State	Statute	Answer
Colorado	Colo. Rev. Stat. §§ 15–11–109; 19–5–211 (2012).	Yes. Adoptee is child of adoptive parents for all inheritance purposes.
Connecticut	Conn. Gen. Stat. Ann. § 45a–731(1)–(3) (West 2012).	Yes. Parent child relationship exists between adoptee and adoptive parents for all purposes, including rights of inheritance between adoptee and adoptee's heirs, on the one hand, and adoptive parents and their issue and other relatives, on the other.
Delaware	Del. Code. Ann. tit. 12 § 508; 13, § 920(b) (2011).	Yes. Collateral or lineal relatives of adoptive parent inherit from adoptee.
District of Columbia	D.C. Code § 16–312 (2012).	Yes. Parent-child relationship exists between adoptee and adopter for all purposes, including mutual rights of inheritance and succession.
Florida	Fla. Stat. Ann. §§ 63.172(1)(c); 732.108 (2012).	Yes. Adoption creates the inheritance relationship between adoptee and adopter and all relatives of adopter that would have existed if adoptee were a legitimate blood descendent of the adopter . . . adoptee is lineal descendent of adopter and is one of the natural kindred of all members of the adopter's family for intestate inheritance purposes.
Georgia	Ga. Code. Ann. § 19–8–19 (2011).	Yes. The relevant statute permits the adoptee all inheritance rights from adoptive parents and adoptive relatives, but

State	Statute	Answer
		does not make reference to reciprocal rights. However, by reason and inference, it is likely that adoptive parents and relatives would have reciprocal inheritance rights from the adoptee.
Hawaii	HAW. REV. STAT. §§ 560:2–109; 578–16* (2011).	Yes.
Idaho	IDAHO CODE ANN. § 16–1508 (2012).	Yes. On adoption, adoptee and adopter have parent-child relationship and all the rights of that relation. Adoptive relatives are not specifically mentioned, but it would follow from the language concerning the creation of a parent-child relationship—and from the reciprocal rights granted to an adoptee—that the adoptive relatives should also inherit from the adoptee.
Illinois	755 ILL. COMP. STAT. 5/2–4(b)** (2011).	Yes. Adoptive parent and adoptive relatives inherit from the adoptee *except* for property which the adoptee has obtained from his biological parents through will, intestacy or gift.
Indiana	IND. CODE ANN. § 29–1–2–8 (2011).	Yes. For all purposes of intestate succession, including succession by, through or from a person, adoptee is treated as biological child of adopting parents.
Iowa	IOWA CODE § 633.223.2 (2012).	Yes. Adoptive parents inherit from and through adoptee. The statute does not make any reference to

State	Statute	Answer
		extended family; however, by reason and by inference, it is arguable that the adoptive family has the right to inherit from the adoptee as well.
Kansas	KAN. STAT. ANN. § 59–2118 (2011).	Yes. Adoptive parent has same "rights" with respect to adoptee as would a birth parent. The statute does not make any reference to extended family; however, by reason and by inference, it is arguable that the adoptive family has the right to inherit from the adoptee as well.
Kentucky	KY. REV. STAT. ANN. § 199.520(2) (2011).	Yes. Adoptee is deemed the child of the adoptive parents for all purposes of intestate inheritance.
Louisiana	LA. CHILD. CODE art. 1218, 1240 (2011).	Yes. Inferred from the statute eliminating rights of the birth parents to inherit from and through the child, it should follow that the adoptive parents inherit from the adopted child.
Maine	ME. REV. STAT. ANN. tit. 18–A § 2–109 (2011).	Yes.
Maryland	MD. CODE ANN., EST. & TRUSTS § 1–207(a) (2012); MD. CODE ANN., FAM. LAW § 5–3B–25 (2012).	Yes. Adoptee is treated as a biological child of the adopting parent or parents; adoptee is child of adopter for all purposes.
Massachusetts	MASS. GEN. LAWS ANN. ch. 210 § 7*** (West 2012).	Yes. Adoptive parents and other adoptive relatives inherit from the adoptee.

State	Statute	Answer
Michigan	MICH. COMP. LAWS ANN. §§ 700.2114 (4)****; 710.60(2) (2012).	Yes. Adopter stands in place of biological parents in all respects.
Minnesota	MINN. STAT. ANN. § 259.59 (West 2012).	Yes. Adoptive parents and their relatives inherit from the adoptee [and vice versa].
Mississippi	MISS. CODE ANN. § 93–17–13***** (2011).	Yes. Adoptive parents and their other children inherit from the adoptee. The statute does not make any reference to extended family; however, by reason and by inference, it is arguable that the adoptive family has the right to inherit from the adoptee as well.
Missouri	MO. ANN. STAT. §§ 474.060; 453.090.3 (2011).	Yes. Adoptive parents inherit from and as parents of adoptees.
Montana	MONT. CODE ANN. §§ 72–2–124; 42–5–202 (2011).	Yes. By stating that adoptive parents and relatives inherit from and through the adoptee, this indicates that adoptive family members may inherit from the issue of the adoptee.
Nebraska	NEB. REV. STAT. §§ 30–2309; 43–110 (2011).	Yes. All rights, duties and legal consequences of parent-child relationship exist between adoptee and adoptive parents.
Nevada	NEV. REV. STAT. § 127.160 (2011).	Yes. Adoptive parents and relatives inherit from adoptee.
New Hampshire	N.H. REV. STAT. ANN. § 170–B:20 (2011).	Yes. Adoptive parents and relatives inherit from the adoptee.

State	Statute	Answer
New Jersey	N.J. STAT. ANN. § 9:3–50 (2012).	Yes. The relevant statute permits the adoptee all inheritance rights from adoptive parents and adoptive relatives, but does not make reference to reciprocal rights. However, by reason and inference, it is likely that adoptive parents and relatives would have reciprocal inheritance rights from the adoptee.
New Mexico	N.M. STAT. ANN. §§ 45–2–114; 32A–5–37 (2011).	Yes. Adoptee inherits from and through adopter and from and through other adopted relatives.
New York	N.Y. DOM. REL. LAW §§ 117.1(c), (g) (2011).	Yes. Adoptee and adoptive parents inherit from and through each other and natural and adopted relatives of the adoptive parent. It is also specifically provided that an adoptive sibling inherits from an adoptee.
North Carolina	N.C. GEN. STAT. § 29–17(c) (2011).	Yes. Adoptive parents and heirs of adoptive parents inherit from and through adoptees.
North Dakota	N.D. CENT. CODE §§ 30.1–04–09; 14–15–14(1)(b) (2011).	Yes. Adoption creates a parent-child relationship between adoptee and adoptive parents for all purposes including inheritance.
Ohio	OHIO REV. CODE ANN. § 3107.15 (A)(2)^ (2011).	Yes. Adoption creates a parent-child relationship between adoptee and adoptive parents for all purposes including inheritance.
Oklahoma	OKLA. STAT. ANN. tit. 10, § 7505– 6.5 (2011).	Yes. Adoptive parents inherit from and through adoptee. Provision omits

State	Statute	Answer
		any direct reference to the rights of adoptive relatives other than adoptive parents; however, by reason and by inference, it is arguable that the adoptive family has the right to inherit from the adoptee as well.
Oregon	OR. REV. STAT. § 112.175(1) (2012).	Yes. Adoptive parents and their issue and kindred take by intestate succession from the adoptee and issue and kindred of adoptee.
Pennsylvania	20 PA. CONS. STAT. ANN. § 2108 (West 2011).	Yes. Adoptee is the issue of the adoptive parent for purposes of inheritance from and through adoptee.
Rhode Island	R.I. GEN. LAWS § 15–7–16 (2011).	Yes. Adoptive parents and their lineal and collateral kindred inherit from the adoptee and descendants of the adoptee.
South Carolina	S.C. CODE ANN. § 62–2–109 (2012).	Yes.
South Dakota	S.D. CODIFIED LAWS §§ 25–6–16; 29A–2–114(b) (2012).	Yes. For purposes of intestate succession by, from or through a person, an adopted individual is the child of that individual's adopting parent or parents and not of that individual's birth parents, except in the case of a stepparent adoption . . . parent child relationship exists between adoptee and adopter and the two have all the rights of that relation.
Tennessee	TENN. CODE ANN. §§ 31–2–105;	Yes. Parent-child relationship exists between

State	Statute	Answer
	36–1–121(b)****** (2012).	adoptive parents and adoptee for all legal consequences . . . lineal and collateral kindred of the adoptive parents and descendants of such kindred inherit from an adoptee, but only as to property acquired post adoption.
Texas	TEX. PROB. CODE ANN. § 40 (2011).	Yes. Adoptive parents and their kindred inherit from and through adoptee.
Utah	UTAH CODE ANN. §§ 75–2–114; 78B–6–139 (2011).	Yes.
Vermont	VT. STAT. ANN. tit. 15A § 1–104 (2012).	Yes. The adoptive parents and their issue inherit from the adoptee and issue of the adoptee.
Virginia	VA. CODE ANN. §§ 63.2–1215; 64.1–5.1 (2012).	Yes. Adoptee is child of adoptive parents for all purposes
Washington	WASH. REV. CODE ANN. § 26.33.260 (2012).	Yes. The relevant statute permits the adoptee all inheritance rights from adoptive parents and adoptive relatives, but does not make reference to reciprocal rights. However, by reason and inference, it is likely that adoptive parents and relatives would have reciprocal inheritance rights from the adoptee.
West Virginia	W. VA. CODE § 48–22–703 (2012).	Yes. Adoptive parents and adoptive relatives inherit from an adoptee.
Wisconsin	WIS. STAT. ANN. §§ 854.20(2); 48.92(1) (2011).	Yes. Adoptee is treated as natural child of his adoptive parents for purposes of intestate succession by, through, or from the adoptee . . . all rights,

State	Statute	Answer
		duties, and legal consequences of the parent-child relationship exist between the adoptee and adoptive parents.
Wyoming	Wyo. Stat. Ann. §§ 2–4–107; 1–22–114 (2011).	Yes. Adoptive parents have all rights with respect to an adoptee as if they were natural parents.

* Haw. Rev. Stat. § 578–16: proposed legislative amendment 2011

** 755 Ill. Comp. Stat. 5/2–4(a): proposed legislative amendment 2011

*** Mass. Gen. Laws Ann. ch. 210, § 7: proposed legislative action 2011

***** Miss. Code Ann. § 93–17–13: proposed legislative amendment 2011

****** Tenn. Code Ann. § 36–1–121(b): proposed legislative amendment 2011

^ Ohio Rev. Code. Ann. § 3107.15(A)(2): limited on constitutional grounds in *Bank One Trust Co. N.A. v. Reynolds*, 173 Ohio App.3d 1, 1 +, 877 N.E.2d 342 (2007)

For all states, adoptive parents inherit from and through their adopted children because the child is treated as if it were their natural child. What is frequently less clear and consequently requires analogous reasoning is if relatives by adoption would inherit through the adopted child, but given the relationship is becoming the equivalent of the natural child of the parents, it follows that relatives would also inherit through the adopted child.

E. Question Five: Stepparent Exception— Is There an Exception to the Traditional Laws of Inheritance if a Child Is Adopted by a Stepparent? If So, What Is the Exception?

State	Statute	Answer
Alabama	ALA. CODE § 43–8–48 (2012).	If the child is adopted by spouse of the natural parent, the adoption has no effect on the child's right to inherit from or through either natural parent.
Alaska	ALASKA STAT. § 25.23.130 (2012).	If a biological parent is the spouse of an adopting parent, adoption does not terminate inheritance rights between adoptee and the biological parent.
Arizona	ARIZ. REV. STAT. ANN. §§ 8–117(b); 14–2109 (2012).	Relationship of adoptee to biological parent who is the spouse of adoptive parents remains unchanged . . . adoption does not affect relationship between adoptee and biological parent who is spouse of adoptive parent.
Arkansas	ARK. CODE ANN. § 9–9–215 (2011).	If one biological parent is the spouse of an individual who adopts the biological parent's child, adoption does not affect inheritance between adopted child and his relatives, on the one hand, and the biological parents and relatives of the biological parent, on the other.
California	CAL. PROB. CODE § 6451(a) (2012).	A parent-child relationship exists between adoptee and biological parent if . . . adoption was by the spouse of either of the biological parents or after the death of either the biological parents . . . a parent-child relationship ex-

State	Statute	Answer
		ists between a child and stepparent, for purposes of intestate inheritance, even if the stepparent has not adopted the child if the relationship began during the child's minority and continued through the parties' joint lifetimes and there is clear and convincing evidence that the stepparent would have adopted the person but for a legal barrier.
Colorado	COLO. REV. STAT. §§ 15–11–109; 19–5–211 (2012).	Natural parent and adoptee retain all right if natural parent is spouse of adoptive parent ... adoption decree or other instrument may specify the rights that are to exist between adoptee and biological parents and relatives.
Connecticut	CONN. GEN. STAT. ANN. § 45a–731(8) (West 2012).	If a child's biological parent has died and the surviving biological parent has, before the other parent's death, married an individual who adopts the child, the adoption has no effect on the inheritance rights between the adoptee and the deceased biological parents and relatives to that point.
Delaware	DEL. CODE ANN. tit. 12 § 508 (2011).	Adoption has no effect on relationship between natural parent who is spouse of an adopting parent; if adoptive parent is a stepparent and married to a biological parent, inheritance rights between adoptee and biological parent and their collateral or lineal relatives are

State	Statute	Answer
		unaffected by the adoption.
District of Columbia	D.C. CODE § 16–312 (2012).	Adoption has no effect on mutual rights of inheritance and succession between adoptee, a biological parent who is spouse of an adopting parent, and collateral relatives.
Florida	FLA. STAT. ANN. § 63.172(1)(b) (2012).	If a biological parent is the spouse of the adoptive parent, the adoption has no effect on inheritance rights between adoptee and the biological parent and relatives.
Georgia	GA. CODE. ANN. § 19–8–19 (2011).	If a biological parent is the spouse of an adopting parent, adoption does not terminate inheritance rights between adoptee and the biological parent and relatives of that parent.
Hawaii	HAW. REV. STAT. §§ 560:2–109; 578–16* (2011).	No right of inheritance through a biological parent who is not a spouse of an adopting parent. If an individual is adopted by person married to a legal parent of the individual, adoption does not terminate inheritance rights between the individual and the legal parent and relatives of the legal parent.
Idaho	—	No statutory provision addresses this point.
Illinois	755 ILL. COMP. STAT. 5/2–4** (2011).	The spouse of any adopting parent is also deemed an adopting parent . . . accordingly, if a biological parent is the spouse of the adoptive parent, the

State	Statute	Answer
		biological parent is deemed an adopter as well. Inheritance between the adoptee and that biological parent (and relatives) would run according to the rules governing inheritance between the adoptee and adoptive relatives.
Indiana	IND. CODE ANN. § 29–1–2–8 (2011).	If biological parent marries adoptive parent, the adoptee inherits from biological parent as though not adopted. No reciprocal specification, but it is implied.
Iowa	IOWA CODE § 633.223.3 (2012).	If spouse of a biological parent is an adopting stepparent, the adoption has no effect on inheritance between the adoptee and the biological parent or heirs of the biological parent.
Kansas	KAN. STAT. ANN. § 59–2118 (2011).	A birth parent who is the spouse of an adopting parent retains the right to inherit from the adoptee. By analogy, it is probable that relatives should also retain the right.
Kentucky	KY. REV. STAT. ANN. § 199.520(2) (2011).	Adoption has no effect on the legal relationship between an adoptee and a biological parent who is the spouse of an adopting parent.
Louisiana	LA. CHILD. CODE ART. 1218, 1240 (2011).	The relationship between the adoptee and a biological parent and relatives of the biological parent is unaffected by an adoption if the biological parent is

State	Statute	Answer
		the spouse of an adoptive parent.
Maine	ME. REV. STAT. ANN. tit. 18–A § 2–109 (2011).	Adoption of a child by the spouse of a natural parent has no effect on the relationship between the child and either natural parent.
Maryland	MD. CODE ANN., EST. & TRUSTS § 1–207(a) (2012).	On adoption by the spouse of a natural parent, the adoptee is still considered the child of that natural parent.
Massachusetts	—	No statutory provision addressing this question.
Michigan	MICH. COMP. LAWS ANN. §§ 700.2114 (2)***; 710.60(2) (2012).	Adoption of a child by the spouse of a natural parent has no effect on the relationship of the child with that parent and does not affect inheritance from the other natural parent.
Minnesota	MINN. STAT. ANN. § 259.59 (West 2012).	Adoption of a child by a stepparent does not in any way change the status relationship between the child and the natural parent who is the spouse of the adoptive parent.
Mississippi	MISS. CODE ANN. § 93–17–13**** (2011).	A biological parent and relatives of the biological parent inherit from an adoptee if the biological parent is the spouse of the adoptive parent.
Missouri	MO. ANN. STAT. § 453.090.2 (2011).	Adoption of a child by spouse of a natural parent has no effect on relationship between child and that natural parent.
Montana	MONT. CODE ANN. §§ 72–2–124; 42–5–202 (2011).	Adoption of a child by the spouse of a natural parent has no effect on the relationship between the

State	Statute	Answer
		child and either natural parent and the adoptee and his or her descendents retain the right to inherit from or through the other natural parent. Inheritance from or through a child by either natural parent or the parent's kindred is precluded, however, unless the natural parent has openly treated the child as the parent's and has not refused to support the child.
Nebraska	NEB. REV. STAT. § 30–2309 (2011).	Adoption of a child by spouse of a natural parent has no effect on relationship between child and that natural parent.
Nevada	NEV. REV. STAT. § 127.160 (2011).	A stepparent adoption does not in any way change the status of the relationship between the child and a natural parent who is the spouse of the stepparent.
New Hampshire	N.H. REV. STAT. ANN. § 170–B:20 (2011).	A stepparent adoption does not alter the rights relative with the relationships between an adoptee and the natural parent who is the spouse of the stepparent.
New Jersey	N.J. STAT. ANN. § 9:3–50 (c)(2012).	Adoption does not terminate any rights based on the relationship between an adoptee and a natural parent who is the spouse of the adoptive parent.
New Mexico	N.M. STAT. ANN. § 45–2–114 (2011).	Adoption of a child by the spouse of a natural parent has no effect on the relationship between the

State	Statute	Answer
		child and the natural parent for purposes of intestate succession, by or through or from a person.
New York	N.Y. Dom. Rel. Law § 117.1(d) (2011).	If a natural parent marries a stepparent who adopts the child, the adoption does not affect the rights of the consenting spouse and the adoptee to inherit from and through each other and the natural and adoptive relatives of that spouse.
North Carolina	N.C. Gen. Stat. §§ 29–17(e)***** (2011).	If a natural parent is the spouse of an adoptive parent, the adoptee is the child of the natural parent for all purposes of intestate succession.
North Dakota	N.D. Cent. Code §§ 30.1–04–09; 14–15–14(1)(a) (2011).	Adoption does not affect inheritance rights between an adoptee and a natural parent and relatives of the natural parent if the natural parent is the spouse of an adopting stepparent. Another statutory provision states that adoption of a child by the spouse of a natural parent has no effect on the relationship between the child and either natural parent (N.D. Cent. Code § 30.1–04–09) . . . An adopted individual is the child of an adopting parent or parents and not of the natural parents, but adoption of a child by the spouse of either natural parent has no effect on the relationship between the child and that natural parent or the

State	Statute	Answer
		right of the child or a descendant of the child to inherit from or through the other natural parent.
Ohio	OHIO REV. CODE ANN. § 3107.15 (A)(1)^ (2011).	Adoption does not affect inheritance rights between an adoptee and a biological or other legal parent or relatives of the parent if the parent is the spouse of an adopting stepparent.
Oklahoma	OKLA. STAT. ANN. tit. 10, § 7505–6.5 (2011).	A biological parent and relatives of the biological parent inherit from an adoptee if the biological parent is the spouse of the adoptive parent.
Oregon	OR. REV. STAT. § 112.175(2)(a) (2012).	If a natural parent is the spouse of an adoptive parent, the adoptee is the child of the natural parent for all purposes of intestate succession.
Pennsylvania	20 PA. CONS. STAT. ANN. § 2108 (West 2011).	If a natural parent is married to the adoptive parent, the adoptee is considered the issue of that natural parent for inheritance purposes.
Rhode Island	R.I. GEN. LAWS § 15–7–17 (2011).	Adoption has no effect on the legal rights of a natural parent with respect to an adoptee if the natural parent is married to the adoptive parent at the time of the adoption decree.
South Carolina	S.C. CODE ANN. § 62–2–109 (2012).	Adoption of a child by the spouse of a natural parent has no effect on the relationship between the child and that natural parent.

State	Statute	Answer
South Dakota	S.D. CODIFIED LAWS §§ 25–6–17; 29A–2–114(b) (2012).	Adoption of a child by spouse of a birth parent has no effect on relationship between child and that birth parent for purposes of intestate succession. Natural parent who is married to stepparent-adopter retains all rights regarding adoptee.
Tennessee	TENN. CODE ANN. § 31–2–105 (2012).	Adoption of a child by spouse of a natural parent has no effect on relationship between child and that natural parent.
Texas	TEX. PROB. CODE ANN. § 40 (2011).	The adoptee retains the right to inherit from and through the natural parent who marries the adopting parent. There is no statutory provision addressing the corresponding question of whether, in the context of a stepparent adoption, the natural parents and their relatives retain the right to inherit from and through the adoptee, though it is safe to assume that relatives would in fact retain the right to inherit.
Utah	UTAH CODE ANN. § 75–2–114 (2011).	Adoption of a child by the spouse of a natural parent or previously-adopting parent has no effect on the relationship between the child and that natural or previously adopting parent. However, the adopted child of a stepparent also gains the right of inheritance through the stepparent, becoming a part of that

State	Statute	Answer
		family for inheritance purposes.
Vermont	VT. STAT. ANN. tit. 15A § 1–104 (2012).	Adoption does not affect inheritance rights by and through a natural parent who is the spouse of an adoptive parent.
Virginia	VA. CODE ANN. § 64.1–5.1 (2012).	Adoption of a child by the spouse of a biological parent has no effect on the relationship between the child and either biological parent
Washington	WASH. REV. CODE ANN. § 26.33.260 (2012).	Adoption has no effect on the inheritance rights of a biological parent who is married to the adoptive parent or has not joined in the petition for adoption. There is no direct reference to relatives aside from the biological parent; however, by analogy and reference, it is safe to infer that inheritance privileges from and through other relatives are reserved as well.
West Virginia	W. VA. CODE § 48–22–703 (2012).	Adoption does not affect inheritance rights between an adoptee and a biological parent who is the spouse of the adoptive parent. Though it does not specifically address the status of inheritance rights between the adoptee and biological relatives other than the biological parent who is the spouse of an adoptive parent; but it can be argued that the exception preserves those inheritance rights as well.

State	Statute	Answer
Wisconsin	WIS. STAT. ANN. §§ 48.92(2); 854.20(2) (2011).	Adoption has no effect on inheritance rights based on the parent-child relationship between an adoptee and a biological parent who is the spouse of an adoptive parent.
Wyoming	WYO. STAT. ANN. § 2–4–107 (2011).	Adoption of a child by the spouse of a natural parent has no effect on the relationship between the child and that natural parent for purposes of inheritance. Thus, the inheritance rights between the adoptee and biological parent will remain intact after adoption.

* HAW. REV. STAT. § 578–16: proposed legislative amendment 2011

** 755 ILL. COMP. STAT. 5/2–4(a): proposed legislative amendment 2011

*** MICH. COMP. LAWS ANN. § 700.2114(4): proposed legislative amendment 2011

**** MISS. CODE ANN. § 93–17–13: proposed legislative amendment 2011

***** N.C. GEN. STAT. § 29–17(e)*****: proposed legislative amendment 2011

^ OHIO REV. CODE. ANN. § 3107.15(A)(2): limited on constitutional grounds in *Bank One Trust Co. N.A. v. Reynolds*, 173 Ohio App.3d 1, 1 + , 877 N.E.2d 342 (2007)

When a child is adopted by the spouse (who is not the natural parent) of a natural parent, the decree of adoption typically has no effect on the relationship between the adopted child and that natural parent. The relationship between the adopted child and the other natural parent is typically terminated, though it is state-specific whether the child can still inherit through the other natural parent and may depend not only on state, but additionally whether the other parent died before the child was adopted by the spouse.

PART THREE

FEDERAL LEGISLATION AFFECTING STATE ADOPTIONS

States exercise primary control over child welfare programs, but in order to qualify for federal funding under certain programs, states must comply with specific federal requirements. The federally funded programs that support state efforts for foster care and adoption activities are found primarily in the Social Security Act and administered by the Department of Health and Human Services. Below is a summary of the Federal legislation spanning the last three decades that has had an impact on foster care and adoption in the fifty states.

I. Indian Child Welfare Act (ICWA) of 1978

25 U.S.C.A. § 1902

In response to the high breakup rate of Indian families by nontribal agencies, ICWA was enacted to establish standards for the placement of Indian children in foster and adoptive homes and to prevent the breakup of Indian families. ICWA established minimum federal standards for the removal of Indian children from their families, required that such children be placed in foster or adoptive homes that reflect Indian culture, created exclusive Tribal jurisdiction overall all Indian custody proceedings when requested by the Tribe or parent and prevented the termination of an Indian parents' parental rights unless the grounds for termination could be proven beyond a reasonable doubt.

II. Federal Adoption Assistance and Child Welfare Act of 1980 (FAACWA)

42 U.S.C.A. § 672

The Adoption Assistance and Child Welfare Act was designed to improve state child welfare and social services programs through open-ended federal funding for qualifying state foster care and adoption assistance programs. The AACWA required states to make these federally funded subsidy payments for foster care maintenance and to parents who adopt a child who is AFDC-eligible (now replaced with the federal Temporary Assistance to Needy Families program) and has special needs. The legislation also conditioned a child's eligibility for federal support upon (1) a judicial finding that remaining at home is contrary to the welfare of the child *and* (2) a showing that the state agency has made "reasonable efforts" to prevent removal, and to take steps to reunite the child, if appropriate. Additionally, AACWA required states to place a child in the least restrictive setting and, if beneficial to the child, one that is close to the parent's home. It further mandated judicial or agency review every six months of a child in any nonpermanent setting for a "best interests of the child" determination, and similarly required the court or agency to determine a future course of action, whether parental reunification, adoption, or continued foster care, within eighteen months after the initial foster care placement.

III. Multiethnic Placement Act of 1994

42 U.S.C. § 5115a(a)(2), repealed by
42 U.S.C. § 1996b.

The Multiethnic Placement Act (MEPA) was enacted as part of title V of the Improving America's Schools Act of 1994 and was aimed at eliminating racial, ethnic and national origin discrimination in the foster care and adoption system. MEPA prohibited state agencies involved in foster care or adoption placements that receive federal funding from delaying, denying or otherwise discriminating on the sole basis of the child or parent's race, ethnicity or natural origin when making placement decisions and likewise banned such discrimination when determining a person's eligibility to become a foster or adoptive parent. Nonetheless, MEPA allowed an agency to consider the cultural, ethnic or racial background of a child and the ability of the adoptive or foster parent to meet the needs of a child with such a background when making a placement. In an effort to strengthen these new provisions, Congress made the failure to comply with MEPA a violation of title VI of the Civil Rights Act and thereby provided a federal cause of action for any person whose rights were violated under the law. But see Small Business and Job Protection Act of 1996 at page 122.

IV. Adoption and Safe Families Act of 1997

42 U.S.C. § 629

As stated earlier, in the 1960s the federal government was concerned with the plight of children in long term foster care and whether there were barriers to adoption. The development of the Model State Act to Free Children for Permanent Placement and the Model State Subsidized Adoption Act reflected those concerns. Thirty years later, n 1997, Congress enacted the Adoption and Safe Families Act (ASFA) with the purpose of promoting the adoption of children in foster care, including provisions that accelerated permanent placement, ensured the safety of abused and neglected children, and modified the "reasonable efforts" standard used by state welfare agencies when making removal and reunification decisions. The ASFA made efforts to accelerate the permanent placement of children by requiring states to initiate a judicial "permanency hearing" for children who had waited at least fifteen of the last twenty-two months in foster care, and allowed the states to free children for adoption more quickly in extreme cases. The Act further encouraged adoptions by providing incentive funds to states that increased adoptions, ensured health coverage for adopted children with special needs, and prohibited states from denying placement of children based upon the geographic location of the adoptive parents. Moreover, Congress required that child welfare agencies consider the "safety of the child" in every step of the case plan and review process. Lastly, the Act clarified the meaning of "reasonable efforts," the efforts that welfare agencies must use to prevent removal and reunification—and did so by mandating the "the child's health and safety" as the paramount concern.

V.   Foster Care Independence Act

42 U.S.C. § 677

In response to the growing foster care population which was leaving the foster care system at age eighteen, Congress enacted the Foster Care Independence Act (FCIA) in 1999 to provide the states with more funding and flexibility to provide programs designed to aid children in the transition from foster care to self-sufficiency. The FCIA created new federal grants to the states that improved the independent living programs for foster youth preparing to living on their own, including those programs that offered education, job training, and employment services, and financial support. The Act also required states to collect data on the services, the youth served, and the outcomes of the youth leaving the foster care system. Congress also provided states with the option of extending Medic-

aid coverage to eighteen to twenty-one year olds
who have been emancipated from foster care.

VI.   Safe and Timely Interstate Placement of Foster Children

42 U.S.C.A. § 673C

The State and Timely Interstate Placement of
Foster Children (STIPFC), enacted in 2006, was
designed to shorten the process and improve the
protections for children who are placed in homes
outside of the state in which they currently live,
oftentimes with other family members. The Act
attempted to speed the placement process where
home studies are required before children can be
moved to out-of-state homes by authorizing grants
in the form of incentive payments to states that
have federally approved plans and that complete
such studies within thirty days. STIPFC also sought
to hasten such interstate placements by allowing
courts to obtain information and testimony from
the other states, thus not requiring interstate travel. The Act also required more caseworker visits to
children in out-of-state foster care placements, mandated the notification of foster parents, preadoptive
parents and relative caregivers of foster children
with respect to certain legal proceedings regarding
the child, and allowed consideration of out-of-state
placements in permanency hearings, case plans and
case reviews.

PART FOUR

INTERCOUNTRY ADOPTION*

Through the years, beginning in the 1960s, American child welfare specialists have been concerned about the exportation of children by certain countries, especially those considered in the third world and about Americans adopting them. Those child welfare experts have expressed the view that exporting countries should really establish their own child welfare systems sufficient to respond to the needs of both parents and children. For the most part, this has not occurred and foreign countries

* For details regarding intercountry adoption including a list of American agencies that deal with foreign adoptions as well as the full text of the Hague Convention on Protection of Children and Co-operation in Respect of Inter-country Adoption see ANN M. HARALAMBIE, HANDLING CHILD CUSTODY, ABUSE AND ADOPTION CASES §§ 14.21–22 (3d ed. 2009). For practical issues and United States immigration law requirements including forms, see JOAN HEIFETZ HOLLINGER, ADOPTION LAW AND PRACTICE §§ 11.01–08; Appendix 11–A (2011). For information regarding specific country's laws regarding intercountry adoption as well as other important domestic matters, see CYNTHIA R. MABRY & LISA KELLY, ADOPTION LAW: THEORY, POLICY AND PRACTICE 411–454 (2d ed. 2010). Of special concern is the United States State Department website, which should be consulted for purposes of gaining insight into specific United States requirements, see <http://adoption.state.gov/index. php>

have been the source for Americans either unwilling
or unable to adopt children in the United States.
Unlike adopting a child in the United States, intercountry adoption usually involves children at least a
few months old and ordinarily not newborns.

From 2007 to 2011 the number of children born
in foreign countries and adopted by American citizens has decreased considerably. In 2007, the number was 19,608 and in 2011 it was 9,320. During
that period, except for the year 2008 when the
number of adoptions was 17,456, and Guatemala
was the country sending the most children to the
United States, China has been the country providing the most children. In 2011, China provided
2,589 children, followed by Ethiopia with 1,727,
Russia with 970, and South Korea with 736. In
2010, when the number of children adopted was
11,059, China led the countries exporting children
to the United States with a total of 3,401, followed
by Ethiopia with 2,513, Russian with 1,082 and
South Korea with 863.

There are two ways of adopting a foreign-born
child. One is to adopt the child in the country of the
child's birth and bring the child to the United
States, in some instances adopting the child again
in the adoptive parents' home jurisdiction. The other is to have the child brought to the United States
and to adopt the child in the adoptive parents'
home jurisdiction. Either way, the United States
Citizenship and Immigration Services (USCIS)
must be consulted for purposes of determining
whether the child qualifies for obtaining an IH–3

visa. In order to fulfill the requirements for that visa, the child must be free for adoption and the adoptive parents must have met the requirements of their own state. If the child is not an orphan, it is very important that prospective adoptive parents be mindful of the necessity of a lawful relinquishment by the birth parents. This is vital for assuring that the child has not been kidnapped or sold, or that the birth parents have not been deceived. Ordinarily, orphans are relinquished by the agency which has cared for them. It is very useful to contact the American Embassy or Consulate in the country from which the prospective adoptive parents wish to obtain a child in order to acquire the most current information about that country's requirements. It may also be helpful to contact the foreign country's embassy or consulate in the United States for additional information.

The process of adopting a child under eighteen from a foreign country is complex and involves a number of issues, like immigration law requirements, that are not found in domestic adoptions. It is not uncommon for an exporting country to change its laws regarding the availability of local children for adoption by foreigners. Intercountry adoption involves the laws of the country of origin, American federal laws, especially immigration and citizenship laws, which must be followed, as well as the law within in the state of the prospective adoptive couple. The Hague Conference on Private International Law adopted the Convention on Protection of Children and Co-operation in Respect of

Intercountry Adoption. That Convention became law in the United States in 2008 and must be followed. The idea behind the Convention is the protection of children and the prevention of their exploitation. In addition to setting up certain organizational requirements like the establishment of a Central Authority, the Convention reflects the best of adoption agency practice that exists in many American jurisdictions. That practice is discussed in the section of this book dealing with agency adoptions and emphasizes the need for protecting children and at the same time recognizing the interests of the birth and the prospective adoptive parents.

Adopting a child from a foreign country should not be taken without serious consideration of the process involved, including the concern for the time for the process to be completed and the necessity for a knowledgeable facilitator or an agency experienced in foreign adoptions. Facilitators can be a lawyer, doctor, or social worker who acts as an intermediary in independent adoptions. Facilitators can also be, and frequently are, private nonprofit international adoption agencies. Using such an agency can be beneficial because of the agency's experience in intercountry adoption. Choosing the agency route is also important if a prospective adoptive couple wishes to adopt a child from a country like Russia that does not allow independent adoptions.

Prospective adoptive parents interested in adopting a foreign child should also expect their expenses to be more than those for a domestic adoption using a child welfare agency. Foreign travel and living in the country of the child's birth for whatever time is required increases the expenses. Subsidized adoption, which is available in cases of adopting "special needs" children in the United States, and is discussed in this book, is unavailable in intercountry adoption because the children are foreign-born and were not placed with the prospective adoptive couple by an American public agency after having been the subject of a dependency proceeding.

Paramount in intercountry adoption is the necessity that prospective adoptive parents recognize that the child may come from an entirely different culture than the adoptive parents. Successful transracial adoptions in the United States are those in which the adoptive parents understand the differences between them and the children and make every effort to make the children feel as comfortable as is humanly possible in fitting into the children's new immediate and extended family and community. Intercountry adoptions share the same goal.

BIBLIOGRAPHY

General

- HOMER H. CLARK JR., THE LAW OF DOMESTIC RELATIONS IN THE UNITED STATES 850–939 (2d ed. 1988).

- IRA MARK ELLMAN, PAUL M. KURTZ, ELIZABETH S. SCOTT, LOIS A. WEITHORN & BRIAN H. BIX, FAMILY LAW: CASES, TEXT, PROBLEMS 1223–1332 (4th ed. 2004).

- FLANGO, VICTOR E. & CAROL R. FLANGO, THE FLOW OF ADOPTION INFORMATION FROM THE STATES (1994).

- ANN M. HARALAMBIE, HANDLING CHILD CUSTODY, ABUSE AND ADOPTION CASES (3d ed. 2009).

- JOAN HEIFETZ HOLLINGER, *Adoption Law, in* 3 THE FUTURE OF CHILDREN: ADOPTION 43 (Richard E. Behrman ed., 1993).

- JOAN HEIFETZ HOLLINGER, ADOPTION LAW AND PRACTICE (Hollinger ed. 2011).

- SANFORD N. Katz, *Dual Systems of Adoption, in* CROSS CURRENTS: FAMILY LAW AND POLICY IN THE US AND ENGLAND 279 (Sanford Katz, John Eekelaar & Mavis Maclean eds., 2000).

- SANFORD N. KATZ, FAMILY LAW IN AMERICA 153–182 (2011).

- SANFORD N. KATZ, JUDICIAL AND STATUTORY TRENDS IN THE LAW OF ADOPTION, 51 GEO. L. J. 64 (1962).

- CYNTHIA R. MABRY & LISA KELLY, ADOPTION LAW: THEORY, POLICY, & PRACTICE (2006).

History

- Joseph Ben–Or, *The Law of Adoption in the United States: Its Massachusetts Origins and the Statue of 1851*, IN NEW ENGLAND HISTORICAL & GENEALOGICAL REGISTER 259 (1986).

- E. Wayne Carp, *A Historical Overview of American Adoption, in Adoption in America*—Historical Perspectives 1–16 (E. Wayne Carp ed. 2002).

- Stephen Cretney, *Legal Adoption of Children, 1900–1973, in* FAMILY LAW IN THE TWENTIETH CENTURY: A HISTORY 596–627 (2003).

- Michael Grossberg, GOVERNING THE HEARTH: LAW AND THE FAMILY IN NINETEENTH-CENTURY AMERICA 268–285 (1985).

- Leo Albert Huard, *The Law of Adoption: Ancient and Modern*, 9 VAND. L. REV. 743 (1956).

- T.E. James, *The Illegitimate and Deprived Child: Legitimation and Adoption, in* A CENTURY OF FAMILY LAW: 1857–1957 39–55 (R.H. Graveson & F.R. Crane eds. 1957).

- Yasuhide Kawashima, *Adoption in Early America*, 20 J. FAM. L. 677 (1981–1982).

- C.M.A. McCauliff, *The First English Adoption Law and Its American Precursors*, 16 SETON HALL L. REV. 656 (1986).

- Stephen B. Presser, *The Historical Background of the American Law of Adoption*, 11 J. FAM. L. 443 (1971).

- T. Richard Witmer, *The Purpose of American Adoption Laws, in* INDEPENDENT ADOPTIONS: A FOL-LOW-UP STUDY 19–43 (Helen L. Witmer, Elizabeth Herzog, Eugene A. Weinstein & Mary E. Sullivan eds., 1963).

- Jamil S. Zainaldin, *The Emergence of a Modern American Family Law: Child Custody, Adoption, & the Courts, 1796–1851*, 73 Nw. U. L. REV. 1038 (1979).

Child Development and Child Protection

- JEANNE M. GIOVANNONI & ROSINA M. BECERRA, DEFINING CHILD ABUSE (1979).

- JOSEPH GOLDSTEIN, ANNA FREUD, & ALBERT J. SOLNIT, THE BEST INTERESTS OF THE CHILD (1996).

- SANFORD N. KATZ, WHEN PARENTS FAIL: THE LAW'S RESPONSE TO FAMILY BREAKDOWN (1971).

- JILL E. KORBIN, CHILD ABUSE & NEGLECT: CROSS-CULTURAL PERSPECTIVES (1981).

- JOHN E.B. MYERS, CHILD PROTECTION IN AMERICA: PAST, PRESENT, AND FUTURE (2006).

Adoption and Assisted Reproduction

- SUSAN FRELICH APPLETON & D. KELLY WEISBERG, ADOPTION AND ASSISTED REPRODUCTION: FAMILIES UNDER CONSTRUCTION (2009).

- CHARLES P. KINDREGAN JR. & MAUREEN MCBRIEN, ASSISTED REPRODUCTIVE TECHNOLOGY: A LAWYER'S GUIDE TO EMERGING LAW AND SCIENCE (2006).

Orphan Trains

- LINDA GORDON, THE GREAT ARIZONA ORPHAN ABDUCTION (1999).

- MARY IRVIN HOLT, THE ORPHAN TRAINS: PLACING OUT IN AMERICA (1992).

- STEPHEN O'CONNOR, ORPHAN TRAINS: THE STORY OF CHARLES LORING BRACE AND THE CHILDREN HE SAVED AND FAILED (2001).

Regulation of Adoption

- Comment, *Moppets on the Market: The Problem of Unregulated Adoptions*, 59 YALE L.J. 715 (1950).

- WILLIAM MEEZAN, SANFORD N. KATZ, & EVA MANOFF RUSSO, ADOPTIONS WITHOUT AGENCIES: A STUDY OF INDEPENDENT ADOPTIONS (1978).

- HELEN WITTMER, ELIZABETH HERZOG, EUGENE WEINSTEIN & MARY SULLIVAN, INDEPENDENT ADOPTIONS: A FOLLOW-UP STUDY (1963).

Secrecy and Adoption Records

- E. WAYNE CARP, FAMILY MATTERS: SECRECY AND DISCLOSURE IN THE HISTORY OF ADOPTION (1998).

- JOHN TRISELOTIS, IN SEARCH OF ORIGINS: THE EXPERIENCES OF ADOPTED PEOPLE (Beacon 1975).

Indian Child Welfare Act

- BJ JONES, MARK TILDEN & KELLY GAINES-STONER, THE INDIAN CHILD WELFARE ACT HANDBOOK: A LEGAL

GUIDE TO THE CUSTODY AND ADOPTION OF NATIVE AMERICAN CHILDREN (2d ed. 2008).

Intercountry Adoption

- DAN H. BERGER, THE INTERNATIONAL ADOPTION SOURCEBOOK (Berger ed. 2008).

- D. MARIANNE BLAIR & MERLE H. WEINER, FAMILY LAW AND POLICY IN THE WORLD COMMUNITY (2003).

- Joan Heifetz Hollinger, *Intercountry Adoption: Legal Requirements and Practical Consideration Sections 11–1 to 11.08 and Section11A, in* ADOPTION LAW AND PRACTICE (2011).

- Linda Silberman, *The Hague Children's Conventions: The Internationalization of Child Law, IN* CROSS CURRENTS: FAMILY LAW AND POLICY IN THE US AND ENGLAND 606–615 (Sanford N. Katz, John Eekelaar & Mavis Maclean eds., 2000).

- http://adoption.state.gov/adoption_process.php

- http://adoption.state.gov/adoption_process/who.php

- http://adoption.state.gov/adoption_process/how.php

- http://adoption.state.gov/country_information/learn_about_a_country.php

- http://adoption.state.gov/us_visa_for_your_child.php

- http://adoption.state.gov/adoption_community.php

INDEX

———————

References are to Pages

———————

293

†